CALVIN COOLIDGE

ENCYCLOPEDIA
of PRESIDENTS

Calvin Coolidge

Thirtieth President of the United States

By Zachary Kent

Consultant: Charles Abele, Ph.D.
Social Studies Instructor
Chicago Public School System

CHILDRENS PRESS ®

CHICAGO

Thirtieth president Calvin Coolidge was born in a rear room of this building.

Library of Congress Cataloging-in-Publication Data

Kent, Zachary.
    Calvin Coolidge / by Zachary Kent.
        p.   cm. — (Encyclopedia of presidents)
    Includes index.
    Summary: Describes the early life, education, and political
career of the president who earned the nickname "Silent Cal."
    ISBN 0-516-01362-9
    1. Coolidge, Calvin, 1872-1933—Juvenile
literature. 2. Presidents—United States—Biography—
Juvenile literature. 3. United States—Politics and
government—1923-1929—Juvenile literature. [1. Coolidge,
Calvin, 1872-1933. 2. Presidents.] I. Title. II. Series.
E792.K46   1988
973.91'5'0924—dc19   88-10880
[B]   CIP
[92]   AC

Picture Acknowledgments

AP/Wide World Photos—4, 5, 6, 10, 17, 29, 30,
37, 44, 45, 57, 58 (top left), 61, 69 (2 photos), 72
(2 photos), 73 (2 photos), 75 (2 photos), 77, 79
(2 photos), 82, 83, 84, 87, 88, 89

The Bettmann Archive—11, 15, 38, 41, 46, 53,
58 (top right and bottom), 60, 63, 64 (bottom),
65

Historical Pictures Service, Chicago—19, 22, 40,
54

Courtesy Library of Congress—24, 55, 56, 80,
85

Courtesy Vermont Historical Society—9, 12, 14,
16, 20, 27, 34, 36, 51, 62, 64 (top), 66

U.S. Bureau of Printing and Engraving—2

Cover design and illustration by Steven Gaston
Dobson

Childrens Press®, Chicago
Copyright ©1988 by Regensteiner Publishing Enterprises, Inc.
All rights reserved. Published simultaneously in Canada.
Printed in the United States of America.
        8 9 10 R 97 96

Calvin Coolidge takes the oath of office on March 4, 1925.

Table of Contents

Chapter 1 Silent Cal 7
Chapter 2 The Shy Vermonter 13
Chapter 3 Up the Political Ladder 31
Chapter 4 The Coolidge Luck 47
Chapter 5 The Roaring Twenties 67
Chapter 6 "I Do Not Choose to Run" 81
Chronology of American History 90
Index 99

Chapter 1

Silent Cal

At two o'clock on the morning of August 3, 1923, an automobile raced into the quiet village of Plymouth Notch, Vermont. It halted in front of a simple white house and three men hurried up the walk and loudly knocked upon the door. Soon an oil lamp glowed in a downstairs bedroom. "What's wanted!" demanded Colonel John Coolidge, sleepily poking his head out the window.

"President Harding is dead," cried out an anxious voice, "and I have a telegram for the Vice President."

For several weeks, Vice-President Calvin Coolidge had been vacationing at his boyhood home. News usually traveled slowly to the remote country cottage because old John Coolidge owned no telephone. On this night, though, members of Vice-President Coolidge's staff had rushed from the neighboring town of Bridgewater. They brought tragic word of Warren G. Harding's sudden death by heart attack.

Immediately John Coolidge climbed upstairs to inform his son. "Calvin! Calvin!" he called out, his voice shaking with emotion.

Coolidge awakened before his father stepped into the bedroom. He and his wife Grace listened with stunned surprise as his father addressed him as "Mr. President." A few words and a glance at the brief telegram quickly brought him the sad news of Harding's death. As he hurriedly dressed, Coolidge grimly thought of his new responsibilities. "I believe I can swing it," he sincerely told himself. Before leaving the room he knelt and prayed for the strength to serve the American people properly.

By the time Coolidge stepped downstairs, Plymouth Notch was bustling with activity. Lights shone up and down the street and curious neighbors stood in their yards. Automobiles rattled into town carrying government officials. Newspapermen gathered in front of the Coolidge house with pens and notebooks in hand.

Quietly and simply, Coolidge first wrote a message of sympathy to Mrs. Harding. Then he issued a brief public statement "to reassure the country" during its time of grief and worry. Next he stepped across the road to the nearest telephone in Miss Florence Cilley's general store. On the telephone, Secretary of State Charles Evans Hughes urged Coolidge to take the presidential oath of office immediately. "It should be taken before a notary," advised Hughes.

In Plymouth Notch, John Coolidge performed the duties of justice of the peace and notary public. Coolidge realized his own father could swear him in.

John Coolidge in the room where he swore in his son as president

At 2:47 A.M. Congressman Porter H. Dale, railroad official L. L. Lane, Coolidge's stenographer, his chauffeur, and other witnesses crowded into the Coolidge family parlor. A flickering kerosene lamp showed the room's plain furnishings: a worn rug, a wood stove, a cluttered desk, a marble-topped table, a rocker, and two straight-back chairs. Dressed in his best black suit, John Coolidge held the presidential oath, taken from a copy of the Constitution and typed onto a sheet of paper. With thin, pursed lips, fifty-one-year-old Calvin Coolidge stood quietly and raised his right hand.

Calvin Coolidge takes the oath of office by the light of a kerosene lamp.

John Coolidge's voice trembled as phrase by phrase he administered the oath. "I, Calvin Coolidge," began his son, repeating the words with his distinct Vermont accent. When he finished he touched his hand to the family Bible which lay opened upon the table and added, "So help me God." Grace Coolidge wept as she realized her husband had just become thirtieth president of the United States. The new president put his arm around her. Wordlessly he shook his father's hand. Then he calmly went back to bed for another three hours' sleep.

News of the dramatic event quickly spread by morning. No U.S. president ever had been sworn in by his own father. The simple ceremony in the rural farmhouse instantly appealed to many people. It seemed perfectly in

"All the News That's Fit to Print."

The New York Times.

EXTRA
8 A.M.
THE WEATHER: Fair Today.

VOL. LXXII....No. 23,932.   ....

NEW YORK, FRIDAY, AUGUST 3, 1923.

TWO CENTS In Greater New York | THREE CENTS FOUR CENTS Within 200 Miles | Elsewhere

PRESIDENT HARDING DIES SUDDENLY; STROKE OF APOPLEXY AT 7:30 P. M.; CALVIN COOLIDGE IS PRESIDENT

COOLIDGE TAKES THE OATH OF OFFICE

His Father, Who Is a Notary Public, Administers It After Form Is Found By Him in His Library.

ANNOUNCES HE WILL FOLLOW THE HARDING POLICIES

Wants All Who Aided Harding to Remain in Office—Roused After Midnight to Be Told the News of the President's Death.

Statement by President Coolidge

Special to The New York Times.

PLYMOUTH, Vt., Aug. 3.—President Calvin Coolidge issued the following statement early this morning:

Reports have reached me, which I fear are correct, that President Harding is gone. The world has lost a great and good man. I mourn his loss. He was my chief and my friend.

It will be my purpose to carry out the policies which he has begun for the service of the American people and for meeting their responsibilities wherever they may arise.

For this purpose I shall seek the co-operation of all those who have been associated with the President during his term of office.

Those who have given their efforts to assist him I wish to remain in office that they may assist me. I have faith that God will direct the destinies of our nation.

It is my intention to remain here until I can secure the correct form of the oath of office, which will be administered by my father...

CALVIN COOLIDGE
Thirtieth President of the United States by the Death of President Harding.

Public Men Voice Tributes To Harding's Worth and Record

WARREN GAMALIEL HARDING
Twenty-ninth President of the United States, Who Died Yesterday in San Francisco.

President's Death Shocks Capital, Which Had Expected Recovery

DEATH STROKE CAME WITHOUT WARNING

Mrs. Harding Was Reading to Her Husband When First Sign Appeared —She Ran for Doctor

BUT NOTHING COULD BE DONE TO REVIVE PATIENT

News of Tragic End Shocks Everybody, Coming After Day Said to Have Been the Best Since His Illness Began a Week Ago.

Special to The New York Times.

SAN FRANCISCO, Aug. 2.—President Harding died at 7:30 o'clock tonight [11:30 o'clock New York time] of a stroke of apoplexy.

The end came suddenly while Mrs. Harding was reading to him from the evening newspaper, and after what had been called the best day he had had since the beginning of his illness exactly one week ago.

A shudder ran through the President's frame and he collapsed.

Mrs. Harding and the two nurses in the sick room knew the end had come, and Mrs. Harding rushed out of the room and asked for Dr. Boone and the others to "come quick."

Dr. Boone and Brig. Gen. Sawyer reached the President before he passed away, but were not able to avert the inevitable.

This formal announcement following soon after told the story of the tragic end:

"The President died at 7:30 P. M. Mrs. Harding and the two nurses, Miss Ruth Powderly and Miss Sue Dosser, were in the room at the time. Mrs. Harding was reading to the President, when, utterly without warning, a slight shudder passed through his frame; he collapsed, and all recognized that the end had come. A stroke of apoplexy was the cause of his death.

"Within a few moments all the President's official party had been summoned."

The *New York Times* announcement of Harding's death and Coolidge's presidency

keeping with Calvin Coolidge's character. In a time of rapid and sometimes wild national change, Coolidge reminded Americans of their old-fashioned values. His tight-lipped shyness had already earned him the nickname "Silent Cal." Soon his forthright nature and common habits, his honesty, self-reliance, and wit endeared him to the country.

Some people claimed the Vermonter owed his steady success to tremendous political luck. Former president William Howard Taft, however, observed with admiration, "He is very self-contained, very simple, very direct, and very shrewd." By hard work and cautious thought, Calvin Coolidge had raised himself from Plymouth Notch farmboy all the way to the U.S. presidency.

11

Chapter 2

The Shy Vermonter

On July 4, 1872, patriotic Americans marched in parades, waved flags, and shot off fireworks. That Independence Day, John Calvin Coolidge was born in the village of Plymouth Notch, Vermont. "My parents," Coolidge recalled, "then lived in a five room, story and a half cottage attached to the post office and general store." His mother, Victoria Moor Coolidge, was a lovely and sensitive woman. "She was of a very light and fair complexion," Coolidge fondly remembered, "with a rich growth of brown hair that had a glint of gold in it." He also observed that "there was a touch of poetry in her nature which made her love to gaze at purple sunsets and watch the evening stars." His father, John Coolidge, kept the general store and worked a farm. In addition he sometimes held local public offices, including tax collector, constable, militia officer, and justice of the peace. Neighbors elected him to represent them in the Vermont state legislature four times. To avoid family confusion, John and Victoria Coolidge dropped their son's first name and always called him Calvin.

Calvin's mother,
Victoria Moor Coolidge

From the very start, Vermont's craggy hills, rocky farms, and hardworking, rugged citizens helped mold Calvin's character. "Vermont is my birthright," he later remarked. "Here one gets close to nature, in the mountains, in the brooks . . . in the lakes [and] fields." Vermonters, he observed, "are happy and contented. They belong to themselves, live within their income, and fear no man." Vermont's old Puritan settlers were honest and spirited, yet kept their feelings to themselves. John Coolidge passed these traits on to his young son.

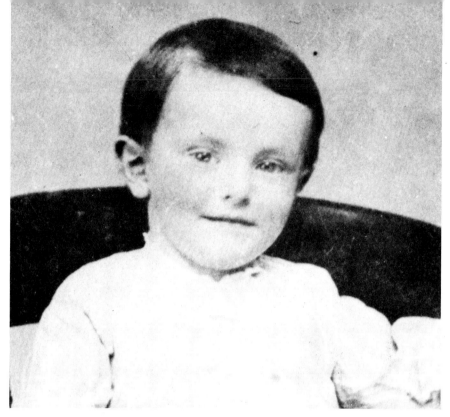

Calvin at the age of three

Being a country boy, Calvin learned to ride horseback. At age three he fell off an old mare and broke his arm. After it mended, his father boosted him back onto the saddle and showed him how to stay there. That same year, Calvin's sister Abigail was born. The birth left Calvin's mother, already in frail health, an invalid.

At the age of five Calvin entered the Plymouth public school. "The little stone school house which had unpainted benches and desks wide enough to seat two," Coolidge later explained, "was attended by about twenty-five scholars." A shy and quiet boy with his mother's delicate features, Calvin proved a good and steady student. One teacher remembered, "He had red hair, blue eyes and freckled face." When Calvin spoke he revealed "a nasal twang that left no doubt as to his New England ancestry."

The little stone schoolhouse where Calvin attended grammar school

Calvin grew more slowly than his classmates. Allergies often caused him to cough and sneeze. Still, he was a healthy lad, able to do his share of farm chores. Calvin looked forward to the maple sugar season every April. "With the coming of the first warm days," he remembered, "we broke a road through the deep snow into the sugar lot, tapped the trees, set the buckets, and brought the sap to the sugar house, where in a heater and pans it was boiled down into syrup to be taken to the house for sugaring off." Proudly John Coolidge later remarked of his son, "It always seemed as though Cal could get more sap out of a maple tree than any other boy I knew."

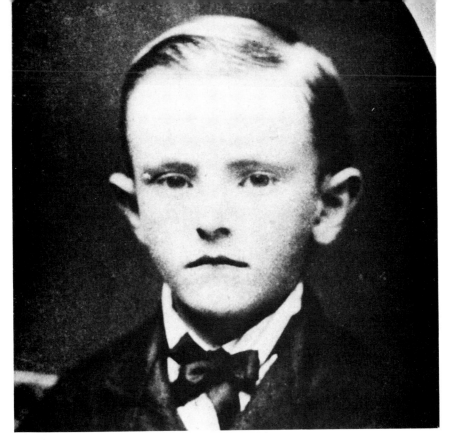

Calvin at the age of seven

Among his other farm work Calvin split firewood, mended fences, and drove the family cattle out to pasture. After the spring planting came sheep-shearing time, which he explained "was followed by getting in the hay, harvesting and threshing of the grain, cutting and husking the corn, digging the potatoes and picking apples."

For fun Calvin attended husking bees, apple-paring bees, singing parties, and local dances. In the winters he ice-skated on frozen ponds, and in the summers he enjoyed swimming and fishing. Some days he visited his Grandfather Calvin Galusha Coolidge's nearby farm. The old man loved practical jokes, and he taught his grandson horseback riding tricks. To impress upon Calvin the value of the land, he deeded the boy forty acres of his own.

Tragedy struck the Coolidge family early in 1885 when Calvin was twelve. A runaway horse injured Victoria Coolidge, and her already fragile health rapidly worsened. There was no hope she would survive. Sadly Calvin revealed, "When she knew that her end was near she called us children to her bedside, where we knelt down to receive her final parting blessing. In an hour she was gone. . . . We laid her away in the blustering snows of March. The greatest grief that can come to a boy came to me. Life was never to seem the same again." All through his adult years Coolidge kept a picture of his mother on his desk.

Another great change occurred in Calvin's life when his father enrolled him in Black River Academy the following year. The private school was located in the town of Ludlow twelve miles away. On a snowy morning in February 1886, Calvin first rode the distance in a horse-drawn sleigh with his father. "As we rounded the brow of the hills," he remembered, "the first rays of the morning sun streamed over our backs and lighted up the glistening snow ahead. I was perfectly certain that I was traveling out of the darkness into the light." "Going to the Academy," he believed, "meant a complete break with the past and entering a new and untried field, larger and more alluring than the past, among unknown scenes and unknown people."

During the next four years Calvin paid for room and board in Ludlow and studied at the Academy along with about 125 other students. Classes in history, mathematics, literature, Latin, and Greek kept Calvin well occupied. On weekends, however, he often walked the long distance to

Calvin Coolidge's sister Abigail, who died at the age of thirteen

Plymouth Notch to visit with his father and sister. Sometimes to earn extra money he worked making toy wagons in Ludlow's carriage shop. Summer vacations, of course, found him doing his chores on the family farm.

As he grew into a teenager Calvin's freckles faded and his red hair turned sandy. When classmates played sports like baseball and football Calvin seldom joined in. "Games did not interest me much," he admitted. "I was rather slender and not so tall as many boys of my age." Instead he made his friends laugh with his dry, witty sense of humor.

Grief struck the Coolidge family again during Calvin's senior year. In March 1890 his sister Abbie suffered serious abdominal pain, probably from a burst appendix. Few doctors then knew how to operate and save a victim of appendicitis. When Abbie's condition became critical, Calvin stayed by her bedside until she died.

Calvin (standing second from left) with his Black River Academy graduating class

For the second time the loss of a loved one plunged the young man into despair. To forget his sadness Calvin turned to his studies. In the spring of 1890 he graduated from Black River Academy along with eight other boys and girls. During the graduation ceremonies Calvin presented an address on "Oratory in History." He hoped to enter Amherst College in the fall, but illness forced him to postpone his plans. After a term at St. Johnsbury Academy in Ludlow, he earned a college entrance certificate.

During the summer of 1891 Calvin and his father rode to Bennington, Vermont, to witness the dedication of a battle monument. Bands blared, soldiers paraded, and public officials joined President Benjamin Harrison on the speaker's platform. Coolidge later recalled, "I heard President Harrison, who was the first President I had ever seen, make an address. As I looked on him and realized that he personally represented the glory and dignity of the United States I wondered how it felt to bear so much responsibility and little thought I should ever know."

Just before Calvin left for Amherst he witnessed his father's marriage to Plymouth Notch schoolteacher Carrie A. Brown. She was "one of the finest women of our neighborhood," Calvin explained. "After being without a mother nearly seven years I was greatly pleased to find in her all the motherly devotion that she could have given me if I had been her own son."

In September 1891 nineteen-year-old Coolidge journeyed south to Amherst, Massachusetts. Like many students at the college, Calvin rented a boardinghouse room near the campus. He lived there frugally and dressed in inexpensive clothes. Walking to classes, many students laughed and shouted hello to one another. But shy and lacking in social charms, Calvin found it difficult to make friends. "I don't seem to get acquainted very fast," he admitted in a letter home. Slim and pale, he rarely took part in sports. Mostly he only watched or took long walks alone through the woods and hills around the town.

In the classroom Calvin also failed to make much of an impression. "During my first two years at Amherst," he revealed, "I studied hard but my marks were only fair. It needed some encouragement from my father for me to continue. In junior year, however, my powers began to increase and my work began to improve." One teacher greatly impressed Coolidge. Philosophy professor Charles E. Garman taught him about the importance and dignity of work. "Our talents are given us in order that we may serve ourselves and our fellow men," Coolidge remembered learning, "yet people are entitled to the rewards of their industry. What they earn is theirs. . . ."

Calvin (left) with some Amherst College classmates in 1895

As his grades improved Calvin also tried to be more sociable. In his junior year he entered his class's comical "Plug Hat Race" wearing a high silk hat. He lost the race but afterwards made a funny speech. "Remember boys," his words concluded, "there are firsts that shall be last and the last first." Gradually Calvin gained a reputation as a wit, and in his senior year members of the college's Phi Gamma Delta social fraternity approached him. "Will you join us?" they asked. Coolidge only replied, "Yes," and soon after became a fraternity brother.

Calvin's college career ended with his graduation *cum laude* (with honors) in the spring of 1895. Seniors who remembered his sense of humor elected Coolidge to give the "Grove Oration" as part of the graduation ceremonies. Perhaps some students thought Calvin's quiet manners and country habits were a source of amusement, but many others laughed aloud at his witty comments.

Calvin had told his father that his goal was to "be of some use in the world." After graduation he decided he could do that best by becoming a lawyer. In September 1895 the law firm of Hammond and Field in North-ampton, Massachusetts, hired him as a clerk. Every day Coolidge pored over the legal books in the office. At night in his rented room he read history books and improved his writing skills. His writing ability became so good that in a national essay contest he won first prize—a gold medal worth $150. Henry Hammond read about the prize in the local newspaper and approached Coolidge at his desk.

"Is that prize yours?" he asked his clerk.

"Yes, sir," answered Coolidge.

"When did you get it?" Hammond questioned.

"About six weeks ago," replied the young man.

"Why didn't you tell us?" the astonished lawyer asked.

"Didn't know you would be interested," Coolidge sim-ply explained.

Calvin's Vermont habit of speaking only when neces-sary, his shyness, and his seriousness soon earned him a reputation as an "odd stick" around Northampton. But he also showed himself to be an excellent law student. On June 29, 1897, he took his Massachusetts bar examination and passed. "My preparation had taken about twenty months," he remembered. "Only after I was finally in possession of my certificate did I notify my father. He had expected that my studies would take another year, and I wanted to surprise him if I succeeded and not disappoint him if I failed. I did not fail. I was just twenty-five years old and very happy."

Calvin Coolidge, the young Northampton lawyer

For seven months Coolidge remained working at Hammond and Field. Then in February 1898 he opened his own law office on Main Street in Northampton. "For my office furniture and a good working library," he revealed, "I paid about $800 from some money I had saved. . . ."

While waiting to build up clients, Coolidge took part in local Republican politics. Impressed by his party loyalty, Northampton Republicans named Coolidge to the city committee. In December 1898 he was elected a city councilman. This post paid no money but brought him into greater contact with influential people. In his free time he visited with his barber, his cobbler, and local shopkeepers. Sitting with these common folk he could relax, and think, and offer a witty remark from time to time.

As Coolidge's reputation for honesty and hard work spread, he obtained more law work. His legal skills and patience enabled him to settle many cases without going to trial. Early in 1900 Coolidge was voted Northampton's city attorney, a position he held for two years. He also served as clerk of the courts for Hampshire County and chairman of the Northampton Republican organization.

Even with these successes Coolidge often worried about money. "If I ever get a woman," he confided to his father, "someone will have to support her." The young lawyer lived in simple style at Robert Weir's boardinghouse in the Round Hill section of Northampton. At the Clarke Institute for the Deaf, located close by, Miss Grace Goodhue worked as a teacher. One day in 1904, as the lovely young woman watered the flowers around the teachers' dormitory she happened to glance up the hill at Weir's boardinghouse. There at a window she noticed Coolidge shaving himself while dressed in his long under-wear and wearing a hat. She burst out laughing at the unusual sight, before turning away with embarrassment. Coolidge overheard her laughter, though, and later asked about her and arranged to be introduced.

Soon he fell in love with the lively, black-haired teacher. He escorted her to dances and card parties. They enjoyed picnics together and country buggy rides. People thought they made a strange couple. Grace's charm and gay spirit touched everyone while Calvin remained silent and kept to himself. Coolidge realized the contrast and joked that "having taught the deaf to hear, Miss Goodhue might perhaps cause the mute to speak."

"From our being together," he later remarked, "we seemed naturally to come to care for each other. . . . We thought we were made for each other." In the summer of 1905 Coolidge turned up at the Goodhue home in Burlington, Vermont.

"Up here on some law business, Mr. Coolidge?" asked Grace's father.

"No," answered Coolidge, "Up here to ask your permission to marry Grace."

"Does she know it?" Mr. Goodhue inquired.

"No, but she soon will," came the reply.

Not long afterwards Coolidge made his straightforward proposal to Grace. "I am going to be married to you," he announced. Cheerfully she accepted.

On October 4, 1905, thirty-three-year-old Calvin Coolidge and twenty-six-year-old Grace Goodhue exchanged marriage vows at her parents' house. The newlyweds honeymooned briefly in Montreal, Canada. When they returned to Northampton they rented half of a two-family house at 21 Massasoit Street for twenty-eight dollars a month.

At about that time Coolidge tried to win a place on the Northampton school board but lost the election. Some people voted against him because he had no children of his own.

"Might give me some time," he briefly commented. A year later in 1906 the Coolidges celebrated the birth of a son they named John. While Coolidge continued work at his law practice, his wife kept their house in order and raised their baby.

Grace Goodhue Coolidge

Coolidge's years of faithful political work paid off in 1906. Republican leaders in Northampton nominated him to be the district's Republican candidate in the fall election for the Massachusetts House of Representatives. By a margin of 264 votes Coolidge won that local contest. In January 1907 he arrived in Boston, the state capital, for the legislative term. In his pocket Coolidge carried a letter of introduction that was given to him by Richard Irwin, an influential Northampton politician. The letter declared of the country lawyer: "Like a singed cat he is better than he looks."

With a valise containing one extra suit, Coolidge rented a room at the inexpensive Adams House hotel. At the statehouse he found his desk among those of the other Massachusetts representatives. Being a newcomer, it is doubtful many of his fellow legislators took much notice of him. But during the session he performed his duties carefully, and the next year satisfied Northampton citizens elected him to a second term. His voting record while in Boston included support of a six-day instead of a seven-day workweek, a call for safer work conditions for women and children, and an effort to grant women the right to vote.

When the 1908 legislature adjourned in June, Coolidge returned home. "I thought I had secured about all the benefit I could by serving two terms," he later explained, "and declined again to be a candidate." The birth of a second son, Calvin, Jr., that April was one reason Coolidge wished to stay in Northampton. Instead of running for state office he agreed to campaign in 1909 for the position of Northampton mayor. "At a party conference," he remembered, "it was determined to ask me to run and I accepted the opportunity, thinking the honor would be one that would please my father, advance me in my profession, and enable me to be of some public service."

Coolidge knew he had to campaign hard that fall in order to beat his popular Democratic opponent. "I called on many voters personally," he revealed, "sent out many letters, spoke at many ward rallies and kept my poise." Many common citizens looked upon Coolidge as a simple man like themselves. In one section of town he secretly

Calvin Coolidge at his desk

spent fifty dollars buying voters drinks and cigars. To other people he often stepped up and frankly said, "I want your vote. I need it. I shall appreciate it." On election day he won the race by 165 votes. "Of all the honors that have come to me," he later remarked, "I still cherish in a very high place the confidence of my friends and neighbors in making me their mayor."

Chapter 3

Up the Political Ladder

Mayor Coolidge served Northampton's citizens by lowering taxes and cutting the town's debt in half. He expanded the police force and the fire department, raised teachers' salaries, and improved the town's streets and sidewalks.

After a second successful though unexciting term as mayor, local Republicans urged Coolidge to run for the Massachusetts state senate. The district included Northampton and the neighboring counties. Modestly Coolidge recalled, "Remaining in one office long did not appeal to me, for I was not seeking a public career. My heart was in the law. I thought a couple of terms in the Massachusetts Senate would be helpful to me, so when our Senator retired I sought his place in the fall of 1911. . . ."

Friends warned Coolidge the contest would be difficult. To this he quietly replied, "It will be just as hard for the other fellow." With the help of the strong local Republican organization Coolidge won the November election.

Coolidge returned to Boston in 1912 and took quarters in the Adams House again. At first he found himself lonesome in the capital. "My old friends in the House were gone," he discovered. Taking up his work in the senate he was named chairman of a Special Conciliation Committee. In this position he tactfully helped end a bitter strike at the Lawrence, Massachusetts, textile mills. As a result, thirty thousand mill workers returned to their jobs with promised pay increases.

Elected to a second term, Coolidge became chairman of the railroad committee and pushed an important bill through the senate. It allowed the New Haven trolley line to extend to Northampton and other western Massachusetts cities. "It was in my second term in the Senate," admitted Coolidge, "that I began to be a force in the Massachusetts Legislature. . . . It was altogether the most enjoyable session I ever spent with any legislative body."

Coolidge managed his advance as a politician without speaking out loudly on public issues. "I made progress," he confided, "because I studied subjects sufficiently to know a little more about them than anyone else on the floor." Working quietly and cautiously, he made few enemies and many friends.

As he began his third term in the senate, the position of president of the senate became available. At forty-one years of age, Coolidge was ready and jumped at the opportunity. Quickly he organized his senate friends and was elected to the position. In his first speech as senate president, Coolidge advised his fellow senators: "Do the days' work. If it be to protect the rights of the weak, whoever objects, do it. If it be to help a powerful corporation better to serve the people, whatever the opposition, do that. . . . We need a broader, firmer, deeper faith in the people—a faith that men desire to do right. . . ." This well-received address soon came to be known as Coolidge's "Have Faith in Massachusetts" speech.

During his two terms as senate president, Coolidge named the senate's committees, assigned bills to the committees, and used his growing influence to pass new laws. In his second term he urged the senators to be brief and managed to cut new legislation by 30 percent. Coolidge's political skill and spirit of cooperation made him a real force in the Massachusetts government.

In the fall of 1915, opportunity again presented itself to Coolidge. The Republican lieutenant governor had decided not to seek another term. "When the situation became apparent to me," Coolidge remembered, "I went to Boston and made the simple statement in the press that I was a candidate for Lieutenant-Governor. . . ." In the campaign that followed, Coolidge worked harder than ever before. Together with the Republican candidate for governor, Samuel McCall, Coolidge toured the state. Coolidge's accented speaking style remained dry, plain, and brief. Unimpressed listeners claimed "McCall could fill any hall in Massachusetts and Coolidge could empty it." Massachusetts Republican leader Murray Crane, however, earlier predicted, "That Yankee twang will be worth a hundred thousand votes." On election day Massachusetts citizens proved Crane correct. Coolidge beat his Democratic rival by more than 52,000 votes.

Governor Samuel McCall (seated) and Lieutenant Governor Calvin Coolidge (left)

In January 1916, Coolidge began the first of his three terms as Massachusetts lieutenant governor. Governor McCall appointed him a member of his advisory council. In addition, Coolidge chaired the state government's finance and pardon committees. Duty required that the lieutenant governor make political speeches throughout the state. In April 1917 the United States entered World War I as an ally of Britain, France, Italy, and other nations in their fight against Germany and Austria-Hungary. Patriotically Coolidge stumped across Massachusetts speaking in support of the war effort.

Gradually the people of the Bay State grew familiar with their lieutenant governor. One citizen saw Coolidge's face and remarked, "It is a pinched drawn face, not hard but anxious, the face of a man perpetually faced with problems too big for him. The face has New England written all over it." A writer named French Strother noticed Coolidge's thoughtfulness. "He is never hurried, never off his guard, never excited."

In the fall of 1918 Coolidge made no secret of his desire to be governor. "Under the custom of promotion in Massachusetts," he later revealed, "a man who did not expect to be advanced would scarcely be willing to be lieutenant governor." Republican leaders in the state trusted Coolidge and willingly awarded him the nomination.

One wealthy Boston merchant in particular, Frank Stearns, greatly admired Coolidge. Stearns eagerly organized Republican support for Coolidge and spent money on campaign pamphlets and posters. During the next weeks Coolidge rode back and forth across the state giving speeches. He admitted to Frank Stearns, however, that his shyness made campaigning difficult. "It's a hard thing for me to play this game," he explained. "In politics one must meet people. . . . When I was a little fellow . . . I would go into a panic if I heard strange voices in the kitchen . . . and the hardest thing in the world was to have to go through the kitchen door and give them a greeting. . . . I'm all right with old friends, but every time I meet a stranger, I've got to go through the old kitchen door, back home, and it's not easy."

Coolidge parades past troops on his way to his inauguration as Massachusetts governor.

In spite of his shyness, in November Massachusetts citizens elected Coolidge governor over his Democratic opponent by a margin of 16,773 votes. From Northampton councilman to the governorship, Coolidge carefully had climbed the political ladder, rung by rung. On New Year's Day, 1919, twenty-one guns boomed a salute on the Boston Commons. Soldiers in historic costumes solemnly paraded, and in the capitol forty-six-year-old Calvin Coolidge took the oath of office. In his inaugural address he advised the people of Massachusetts: "We must steadily advance. Each individual must have the rewards and opportunities worthy of the character of our citizenship, a broader recognition of his worth and a larger liberty, protected by order — and always under the law."

Troops returning home from World War I

Coolidge still lived modestly at the Adams House. In honor of his new position, though, he rented an additional room and expanded his quarters into a suite. On official occasions Grace Coolidge joined her husband in Boston. Most often, however, she remained in Northampton raising the two Coolidge boys.

World War I had ended in November 1918 with an Allied victory. In April troop ships docked in Boston Harbor. During a huge parade Governor Coolidge, from his place on a reviewing stand, welcomed the first triumphant American soldiers home from France.

New York City, 1917: Women demonstrate for lower food prices.

The returning veterans needed places to live. Governor Coolidge appointed a state commission to study the housing shortage. He also encouraged new laws to keep landlords from raising rents too high. Through the next months Coolidge continued to show his interest in the welfare of the Massachusetts people. He approved a law raising workmen's compensation allowances and another limiting the workweek of women and children to forty-eight hours. He urged pay increases for factory laborers and schoolteachers, and he hired skilled and honest citizens to fill state offices.

Coolidge's term of office proceeded smoothly until trouble erupted in the Boston Police Department in the summer of 1919. For years the city's policemen had complained of poor work conditions. They labored long hours at low pay out of dirty, shabby station houses. Many policemen angrily formed a trade union in order to win better treatment.

In response, Boston Police Commissioner Edwin Curtis announced that "a police officer cannot consistently belong to a union and perform his sworn duty." Commissioner Curtis refused to recognize the new policemen's union and put nineteen of its leaders on trial. Furiously other officers threatened a general strike.

As these troubles intensified, Governor Coolidge issued a statement to newspaper reporters:

"Understand that I do not approve of any strike. But can you blame the police for feeling as they do when they get less than a street car conductor?"

In spite of Coolidge's attempts to smooth the situation, on September 9, 1919, 75 percent of Boston's police officers (1,117 men) abruptly walked off the job. Frightened citizens locked their doors and shuttered their windows and waited for the worst. Without the police there was no one to protect them.

After sunset, wild, lawless mobs filled the city streets. Men openly gambled with dice on the Boston Commons. Young hoodlums loudly yelled, threw rocks, and overturned fruit stands. After midnight, riots burst out and looters broke into stores. Decent citizens unlucky enough to be caught outside were robbed.

Coolidge inspects guardsmen during the Boston police strike.

The next day Mayor Andrew Peters called out the state militia stationed in Boston to help keep the peace. That night riots raged again. National guard officers on horseback galloped back and forth shouting orders. Enlisted militiamen with fixed bayonets fought to restore order. On September 11 the headlines of the Boston *Herald* blared, "RIOTS AND BLOODSHED IN CITY AS STATE GUARD QUELLS MOB." In South Boston a volley of gunfire had killed two men and had wounded nine others.

To prevent a third night of violence, Governor Coolidge at last stepped into the affair. Taking charge, he ordered out the rest of Massachusetts's national guardsmen. Through the night of September 11 these soldiers patroled until calm at last returned to the city. Afterwards Coolidge

American Federation of Labor leader Samuel Gompers

expressed his confidence in the decisions of Commissioner Curtis and agreed the striking policemen should be fired. Union leader Samuel Gompers of the American Federation of Labor strongly objected to the governor's stand. But Coolidge insisted, "There is no right to strike against the public safety by anybody, anywhere, any time!"

Newspapers throughout the country reprinted these bold words. During a time of widespread labor worries many Americans greatly admired Coolidge's tough attitude. Newspaper editorials praised the governor. Thousands of supportive letters and telegrams poured into his office. Even President Woodrow Wilson issued a statement congratulating him. As a result of the Boston Police Strike, Coolidge suddenly emerged as a national hero.

"The law . . . should be supreme." That was the issue upon which Coolidge based his popular fall reelection campaign. Later he remarked, "Many of the wage-earners both organized and unorganized, who knew I had always treated them fairly, must have supported me, for I won by 125,101 votes." Although Coolidge was very pleased with the results, he restrained himself from showing his feelings. "The Coolidges never slop over," he stated.

The important event of Coolidge's second term was a required reorganization of the Massachusetts state government. With courage Coolidge reduced the number of state bureaus from 118 to 20. Many bureau chiefs voiced anger when they were being demoted, but Coolidge refused to shirk his duty. Afterwards the governor told his secretary, "I am glad it is done! It is the worst job I ever had to do!"

In June 1920, Republicans gathered in Chicago to select a presidential candidate at their national convention. Many Massachusetts Republicans wished to present Coolidge to the convention as a "favorite son" candidate from their state. Frank Stearns sent Coolidge's book of collected speeches, *Have Faith in Massachusetts*, to every convention delegate. Coolidge's record of faithful Republican service appealed to some delegates. Others remembered the Massachusetts governor as the hero of the Boston police strike.

Voices echoed through the Chicago Coliseum on June 11 as delegates rose to make nominating speeches. General Leonard Wood, Senator Hiram Johnson of California, and Illinois governor Frank Lowden were among the names nominated. During these proceedings Frederick Gillet, a congressman from Massachusetts, spoke in behalf of Calvin Coolidge.

"His character is as firm as the mountains of his native state," proclaimed Gillet. "Like them his head is above the clouds and he stands unshaken amid the tumult and the storm." The crowd applauded politely but without the deep enthusiasm they had given other candidates.

At five o'clock the voting began. On the first ballot Coolidge received thirty-four votes, mostly from Massachusetts delegates. This total lagged far behind those given for Wood, Johnson, and Lowden. During following ballots Coolidge's support weakened. But no candidate could win a majority of votes. Utah senator Reed Smoot muttered, "There's going to be a deadlock, and we'll have to work out some solution."

When the convention recessed that night, several powerful senators met in rooms at the Blackstone Hotel. These men wished to pick a candidate who would seem strong but would be easy to control. Together in their "smoke-filled" hotel rooms they finally agreed to support the candidacy of Ohio senator Warren G. Harding. As a result of this secret bargaining, the next day Harding won the Republican presidential nomination on the tenth ballot.

In Boston, Coolidge learned of the convention's choice with disappointment. He had no desire to compete for the vice-presidential nomination, and he imagined his political career had reached its end.

At his rooms in the Adams House he sat with his wife and discussed their future.

The 1920 Republican national convention at the Chicago Coliseum

Meanwhile in Chicago, the same senators who had chosen Harding wished to make Wisconsin senator Irvine L. Lenroot his vice-presidential running mate. But many delegates resented the fact that these senators exerted so much control over the nominations. The Oregon delegates decided to name a candidate to compete with Lenroot. "I name for the exalted office of Vice President," hoarsely shouted Oregon delegate Wallace McCamant above the convention noise, "Governor Calvin Coolidge, of Massachusetts."

Delegates from other states quickly jumped to their feet and seconded the nomination. Through the great auditorium, voices cried out, "Coolidge! Coolidge!" Men suddenly waved banners with the Coolidge motto: "Law

Harding (center) and Coolidge (right) discuss campaign plans with the Republican chairman.

and Order." In an exciting turnaround, it instantly seemed that Coolidge would be impossible to beat. The Republican Senate leaders watched unhappily as the convention overwhelmingly voted to give Coolidge the vice-presidential nomination.

At the Adams House in Boston, the telephone rang; when Coolidge answered, he learned of McCamant's surprising nominating speech. A little while later the telephone rang again. Coolidge picked it up and listened a moment before hanging up.

"Nominated for vice president," he informed his wife.

"You aren't going to take it, are you?" Grace Coolidge asked.

"I suppose I'll have to," he answered dutifully.

Chapter 4

The Coolidge Luck

Realizing the honor bestowed upon him, Coolidge happily joined the 1920 Republican campaign ticket. To oppose Harding and Coolidge, the Democrats chose Ohio governor James M. Cox to run for president and Assistant Secretary of the Navy Franklin D. Roosevelt as vice-presidential candidate.

Coolidge seemed especially slight and meek when photographers snapped pictures of him standing beside big, darkly handsome Warren G. Harding. The two men got along well, however, and Coolidge cheerfully threw himself into the election contest.

Many Americans had tired of the policies of the previous Democratic administration and decided to vote Republican in 1920. As a result of the Nineteenth Amendment to the Constitution, women were allowed to vote nationally for the first time. Harding's good looks were said to help him attract some of the female vote. Whether that were true or not, on election day, November 2, 1920, by a margin of almost two to one, Harding and Coolidge beat their opponents in an overwhelming victory.

Opposite page: Coolidge's
official presidential portrait

Coolidge had won his eighteenth election. Early in 1921 he journeyed with his family to Washington, D.C., and rented a suite at the New Willard Hotel. On the crisp, bright day of March 4 Coolidge rode past cheering crowds in the inaugural parade to the Capitol. In the Senate chamber he solemnly took the oath of office as U.S. vice-president. After a brief address praising Congress, Vice-President Coolidge joined the officials assembled on the Capitol's east portico to witness Harding's swearing-in ceremony as president.

As the new administration began, President Harding paid his vice-president a compliment by inviting him to cabinet meetings in the White House. Although Coolidge regularly attended, he rarely offered much advice on national affairs.

As president of the U.S. Senate, Coolidge dutifully kept the senators in order and Senate business running smoothly. The vice-president's cool and quiet nature soon became well known to the members of the chamber. One day several senators got into a yelling match. A senior senator turned to Coolidge and requested he pound his gavel and restore order. Amid the confused shouting the vice-president calmly replied, "I will if they become really excited."

Duty also required that Coolidge present the Harding administration's views in public speeches. Although he seldom enjoyed this chore, he remembered, "I spoke some and lectured some. This took me about the country in travels that reached from Maine to California. . . . I was getting acquainted. Aside from speeches I did little writing, but I read a great deal and listened much."

Clearly Coolidge preferred to listen rather than to talk. Stories of his tight-lipped behavior circulated throughout Washington until he became famous as "Silent Cal."

One day Channing H. Cox, the new governor of Massachusetts, visited the vice-president in his office. Cox wondered how Coolidge had been able to see so many callers every day while governor and still leave work at five o'clock. Cox often had to stay at his desk until after 9:00 P.M. "How come the difference?" he asked Coolidge. "You talk back," dryly remarked the vice-president.

On another occasion, Coolidge presided at a ceremony to lay a cornerstone for a new public building. The vice-president dug up the customary shovelful of earth. Then workers laid the cornerstone. When that was done the crowd waited, expecting to hear a speech, but the vice-president said nothing. Finally, the master of ceremonies approached him and asked for a few words. In response Coolidge gazed at the freshly turned-up dirt at his feet and after a moment pointed out, "There's—a—mighty fine fishworm."

The vice-president received many social invitations and enjoyed the attention paid him in Washington. But his shyness and wit often got the better of him at dinner parties, too. At one function a young woman asked him why he attended so many luncheons and dinners. "Got to eat somewhere," Coolidge plainly replied. Another time a society woman sat down next to him at dinner. "You must talk to me, Mr. Coolidge," she gushed. "I made a bet today that I could get more than two words out of you." Coolidge eyed the woman briefly before answering, "You lose."

Most people in Washington believed Coolidge was an unusual character. Few of them thought, however, that he had much of a political future. In the senators' restaurant one day, a visiting representative noticed Vice-President Coolidge eating alone and unnoticed at a corner table. "Is that how you treat your presiding officer?" the congressman asked Senator Edwin Ladd. "Nobody has anything to do with him," sadly answered the senator. "After this, of course, he's through."

In Massachusetts, though, people regarded Coolidge differently. Year after year they had watched his steady political progress with wonder. Those who failed to recognize Coolidge's real political abilities talked openly of "Coolidge Luck." After Coolidge's vice-presidential nomination, one Boston reporter was overheard making bets that Harding, if elected, would be assassinated within two years. "I am simply telling you what I know," he excitedly predicted. "I know Cal Coolidge inside and out. He is the luckiest [fellow] in the whole world!" After a visit to Massachusetts in 1921, an Illinois politician wrote, "Up in Boston Coolidge's friends seem to all think that Harding will not live his term out and that Cal's luck will pursue him into the White House."

In the summer of 1923 Coolidge said good-bye to President Harding. He journeyed north to Vermont on a vacation, while Harding boarded a train that carried him out west on a relaxed speaking tour. After visiting Alaska, Harding started down the Pacific coast. In Seattle, the president unexpectedly fell ill. Doctors believed he suffered food poisoning from eating spoiled crabmeat.

The Coolidge home in Plymouth Notch, where Calvin Coolidge became president

Continuing on to San Francisco, the president rested several days and his health seemed to improve. No one was prepared for the stunning news when a heart attack suddenly killed Harding at 7:30 P.M. on August 2.

"My God! That means Coolidge is President!" exclaimed Massachusetts senator Henry Cabot Lodge when reporters brought him the word.

In Plymouth Notch, Coolidge spent the afternoon of August 2 operating a horse rake to gather hay in a neighbor's field. In the evening he ate a hearty meal and at nine o'clock retired upstairs to bed in his father's house. It was well after midnight when an automobile carried three excited men into the crossroads village. Some hurried steps, a few loud knocks on the door, and soon old John Coolidge learned the startling news that most of the nation already knew by then. He hastened to tell his son.

"On the night of August 2, 1923," recalled Coolidge, "I was awakened by my father coming up the stairs calling my name. I noticed that his voice trembled. As the only times I had ever observed that before were when death had visited our family, I knew that something of the gravest nature had occurred." In another moment John Coolidge entered the bedroom and addressed his son as "Mr. President." "He placed in my hands an official report," explained Coolidge, "and told me that President Harding had just passed away."

Coolidge quickly dressed, as all of Plymouth Notch became aware of the news. Soon he realized that his father, as a notary public, could swear him in as president. "The oath," Coolidge revealed afterwards, "was taken in what we always called the sitting room by the light of the kerosene lamp, which was the most modern form of lighting that had then reached the neighborhood." After repeating the solemn presidential oath before a few witnesses in the simple room, Coolidge signed the typewritten copy and his father affixed his official notary seal. Then thirtieth U.S. president Calvin Coolidge returned to bed for another few hours' rest.

Although he understood the enormous challenges before him, Coolidge was unlikely to change his basic country character. Fifteen-year-old Calvin Coolidge, Jr., was working in a Connecticut tobacco field that summer. When the news arrived about his father, a fellow laborer remarked, "If my father was President I would not work in a tobacco field"—to which young Calvin answered, "If my father were your father, you would."

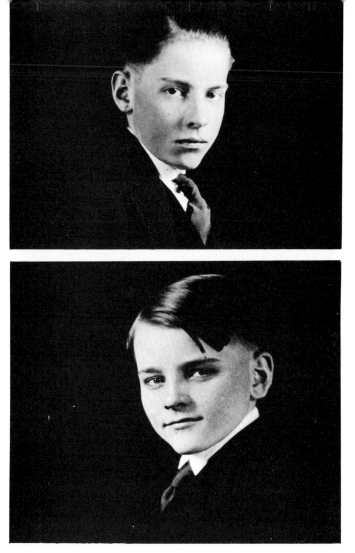

Coolidge's sons, John (top) and Calvin, Jr. (bottom)

On the morning of August 3, the new president prepared to return to Washington. As he left his father's house he noticed a loose stone step leading to the porch. "Better have that fixed," he mentioned to his father. Before the president's automobile had carried him very far, Coolidge ordered it stopped. At the family cemetery he got out and silently stood at his mother's grave for a while. "Some way, that morning," he later explained, "she seemed very near to me."

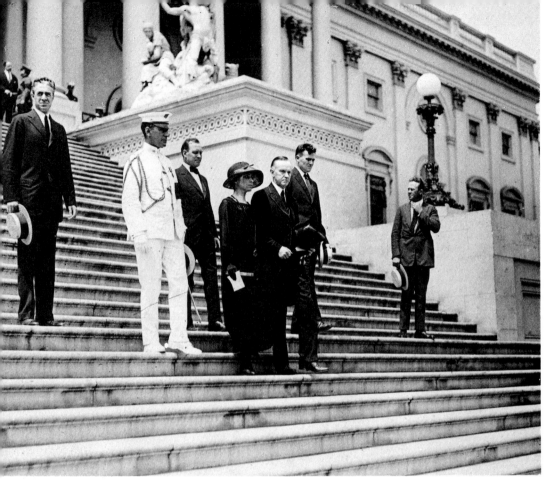

President and Mrs. Coolidge leaving the Capitol after Harding's memorial service

All the nation mourned the death of President Harding. Coolidge took part in the sad funeral ceremonies and insisted that Mrs. Harding not be rushed as she assembled her possessions to leave the White House. When Coolidge did move in several days later, however, he instructed White House usher Ike Hoover, "I want things as they used to be—before!" President Harding often had hosted late-night poker parties. Old cronies smoked cigars, told crude jokes, and drank whiskey, even though the 1919 Volstead Act outlawed alcohol in the United States. Clearly President Coolidge intended to restore dignity to the White House.

Coolidge with Calvin, Jr. (left) and John (right), on June 30, 1924.
Calvin, Jr. died a week later, on July 7, 1924.

Alice Roosevelt Longworth, daughter of President Theodore Roosevelt, remarked that the first time she "went to the White House after the Coolidges were there, the atmosphere was as different as a New England front parlor is from a back room in a speakeasy." During his first few days in the White House, Coolidge even relaxed in the evening on the front porch in a rocking chair. Staring crowds outside the fence and traffic jams in the street forced him to give up that quaint country habit.

Coolidge spent a lot of time exploring his new White House surroundings. He stalked the halls and examined all of the rooms and even the attic. In the kitchen he counted hams and went over the daily menus. In his office he prankishly enjoyed ringing the bells on his desk in order to see his staff come running.

President Coolidge poses with his cabinet.

For the most part Coolidge took his duties as president seriously. He studied national affairs and sought the advice of such men as former president William Howard Taft, now chief justice of the Supreme Court. Ike Hoover observed that "President Coolidge was different from all the rest. He seemed always to be watching, rather suspicious lest something be 'put over' on him."

Coolidge intended to keep all of the members of Harding's cabinet in office and continue Harding's policies. Soon after he became president, however, Americans learned of the Teapot Dome scandals. The U.S. government owned some western oil lands, including one rise of land called Teapot Dome in Wyoming. Private companies wished to develop these oil reserves and heavily bribed Secretary of the Interior Albert B. Fall to make two of them available for lease. With the help of Secretary of the

Secretary of the Navy Edwin Denby, a Teapot Dome conspirator

Navy Edwin Denby and Attorney General Harry M. Daugherty, Fall carried out this illegal activity in 1921.

As stories about Teapot Dome circulated, the U.S. Senate ordered an investigation. Joining outraged Americans, Coolidge issued a public statement urging, "Let the guilty be punished." Eventually Interior Secretary Fall was convicted of bribery, fined $100,000, and sentenced to a year in prison. Navy Secretary Denby resigned in shame. Idaho senator William Borah strongly advised Coolidge to fire Attorney General Daugherty, too. At the White House, Coolidge called in both Borah and Daugherty. Borah confronted the Attorney General with his crime and Daugherty angrily yelled his defense. All the while the president silently listened until Daugherty stormed out of the room. "I reckon you are right," Coolidge commented at last to the Idaho senator. In time Coolidge demanded Daugherty's resignation.

Above: Two government officials involved in the Teapot Dome scandal: Secretary of the Interior Albert B. Fall (left) and U.S. Attorney General Harry M. Daugherty (right)

Left: A 1922 cartoon showing the "explosion" of the Teapot Dome

Coolidge's careful handling of the Teapot Dome affair brought him added respect. No one doubted his personal honesty, and the huge scandal failed to hurt his administration. Although many Americans thought he was an odd character, they welcomed his style of politics.

"The chief business of America is business," Coolidge announced early in 1924. He did not believe in government regulation, and as a result businesses boomed throughout the nation. The country "wanted nothing done" while Coolidge was in the White House, someone remarked, "and he done it."

"Four-fifths of all our troubles in this life," commented Coolidge, "would disappear if we would only sit down and keep still." During 1923 and 1924 Coolidge kept still and let America prosper.

As the national election of 1924 approached, most Republican leaders agreed Calvin Coolidge deserved the presidential nomination. Coolidge had saved the Republicans from total embarrassment during the Teapot Dome scandal and it seemed that, as Chief Justice Taft remarked, "the Republican party has no chance without him."

In June 1924 Republicans gathered in Cleveland, Ohio, for the first national party convention ever to be broadcast on radio. Listeners at home heard speaker after speaker praise Coolidge. One Republican, for example, proclaimed that Coolidge "never wasted any time, never wasted any words, and never wasted any public money." On the first ballot Coolidge easily won the nomination of his party. For the vice-presidential candidate, delegates picked Charles G. Dawes of Illinois.

REPUBLICAN STANDARD BEARERS
1924

FOR PRESIDENT.

FOR VICE-PRESIDENT.

– TWO GREAT AMERICANS –

A 1924 election poster for Coolidge and Dawes

Democrats meeting two weeks later at their convention in New York City found themselves unable to agree on a candidate. For ten days delegates met in the stifling hot auditorium of Madison Square Garden. Finally, after an all-time record of 103 ballots, they nominated compromise candidate John W. Davis, a wealthy lawyer from West Virginia.

Some liberal Americans claimed both Coolidge and Davis too closely represented conservative business interests. Meeting in Cleveland in July, the Progressive party nominated Wisconsin senator Robert La Follette as their presidential choice.

Progressive party candidate Robert M. La Follette

The 1924 Republican campaign got under way with banners and posters announcing the slogan: "Keep Cool with Coolidge!" Before the contest advanced too far, however, personal tragedy struck the Coolidge family. After playing tennis on the south grounds of the White House one day, sixteen-year-old Calvin, Jr., discovered a blister on his toe. In a few days an infection developed and the boy grew feverish. While doctors worked to reverse the blood poisoning, Coolidge often visited his son's bedside. On July 7, however, the boy died. With deep grief Coolidge later remembered, "In his suffering he was asking me to make him well. I could not. When he went the power and the glory of the Presidency went with him."

Left to right: Son John, wife Grace, father John, Coolidge, and son Calvin, Jr.

Republican leaders continued the 1924 campaign while Coolidge mourned the loss of his son. When Coolidge finally did hit the campaign trail, he exhibited his typical silent character. One day a group of reporters gathered around him. "Have you any statement on the campaign?" asked one. "No," replied Coolidge. Another newsman asked, "Can you tell us something about the world situation?" "No," he responded again. "Any information about Prohibition?" requested a third man. "No," came his final answer. Then as the disappointed reporters turned to leave Coolidge solemnly said, "Now, remember—don't quote me."

President Coolidge and Vice-President Dawes

On election day, November 4, 1924, Americans walked to their polling places and voted for president. During Calvin Coolidge's year as president the national economy had thrived, so most people guessed he would be an easy winner. Sure enough, when the votes were tallied, they revealed:

	Popular Vote	Electoral Vote
Calvin Coolidge	15,725,016	382
John W. Davis	8,385,586	136
Robert La Follette	4,822,856	13

Republicans and business leaders cheered Coolidge's tremendous victory. Commented newspaper editor William Allen White, "In a fat and happy world, Coolidge is the man of the hour. Why tempt fate by opposing him?"

Above: Coolidge with his father and stepmother. Below: Grace Coolidge
with sons John and Calvin, Jr. Opposite page: Grace Coolidge

The president and vice-president with their wives on inauguration day

Chapter 5

The Roaring Twenties

March 4, 1925, dawned clear and mild in Washington, D.C. Along Pennsylvania Avenue enthusiastic throngs pressed close to watch the inaugural parade. Marching brass bands blared patriotic tunes. Troops of cavalrymen trotted by on shining horses. The crowd gazed at the line of automobiles that motored past, filled with government leaders and foreign diplomats. When the people finally spied the car carrying fifty-two-year-old Calvin Coolidge, they loudly cheered and waved flags.

At noon Coolidge stepped out onto the Capitol's east portico. With a hand upon his grandfather's Bible, he repeated the oath administered by Chief Justice Taft. In a low voice he swore to "preserve, protect and defend" the laws of the U.S. Constitution. Then he turned to the radio microphones to deliver his inaugural address. "Here stands our country, an example of tranquillity at home," he told his audience. "We appear to be entering an era of prosperity which is gradually reaching into every part of the nation."

During President Coolidge's full four-year term, the country certainly experienced prosperity. The times were marked by such confident, carefree feelings and such rapid social change that the entire decade came to be called "The Roaring Twenties."

The American soldiers who returned home from World War I had seen brutal, bloody fighting in Europe. They understood the value of human life and vowed to get the most out of it. Every American family wanted to own a telephone, a radio, a phonograph, and a washing machine. The mass production on assembly lines of Henry Ford's Model T automobile made the "Tin Lizzie" affordable to almost everyone.

The Volstead Act still prohibited the sale of alcohol. But Prohibition failed to keep many Americans from drinking. Some people concocted "bathtub gin" at home. Others visited secret saloons called speakeasies, where they could drink illegally. In the South, some country folk worked by the light of the moon and distilled "moonshine" to drink. Across the North, mobsters like Chicago's Al Capone smuggled alcohol into the country, sometimes battling with police or rival gangs while doing so.

In 1925, biology teacher John Scopes taught Darwin's theory of evolution at his Tennessee school. To suggest that humans might have descended from apes instead of from the Bible's Adam and Eve defied Tennessee law. During his trial Scopes was ably defended in court by lawyer Clarence Darrow. Although Scopes lost his case and paid a fine, his stand helped broaden educational thinking in the United States.

Above: Tennessee biology teacher John T. Scopes (right).   Below: Defense attorney
Clarence Darrow (left) and prosecuting attorney William Jennings Bryan (right)

Americans found many ways to entertain themselves in the 1920s. In New York, baseball fans yelled themselves hoarse when Yankee star Babe Ruth hit sixty home runs in 1927. At movie theaters that same year, audiences excitedly listened to Al Jolson performing in *The Jazz Singer*, the first talking motion picture. On Saturday nights, young fashion-conscious women with bobbed hair and short skirts danced the latest craze — the Charleston — with their boyfriends, some of whom wore heavy raccoon coats.

Advances in aviation made Americans cheer with pride. In May 1926, Richard Byrd and Floyd Bennett became the first men to fly over the North Pole. Three years later Byrd flew over the South Pole, too. The greatest event of the day, however, was Charles Lindbergh's historic solo flight across the Atlantic. In his little plane, *The Spirit of St. Louis*, Lindbergh lifted off from New York on May 20, 1927. Thirty-three-and-a-half hours later, French citizens crowded Le Bourget Airfield as the exhausted pilot landed in Paris. Young and handsome "Lucky Lindy" became an instant national hero. Upon his return to America, ticker tape fluttered thickly in the air as New Yorkers threw a tremendous parade in Lindbergh's honor.

While the country giddily roared ahead, Coolidge impressed Americans with his apparent inactivity. The president generally arose early each day and often invited congressmen to breakfast with him. Afterwards he routinely worked in his office, answering mail and receiving callers. Following lunch he took a nap and then resumed work another few hours before quitting for the day. Usually he climbed into bed by ten o'clock.

With his nap included, Coolidge often slept eleven hours a day. People openly joked about this habit. "A remarkable man, a really remarkable man," complained editor H. L. Mencken. "Nero fiddled while Rome burned, but Coolidge only snores." One night Coolidge attended the theater where the Marx Brothers were acting in the comedy *Animal Crackers*. Groucho Marx noticed him in the audience and called out, "Isn't it past your bedtime, Calvin?"

Coolidge maintained a healthy sense of humor about his sleeping habits. He even teased himself after napping one afternoon. When a White House staff member awakened him, the president smiled and asked, "Is the country still here?"

Coolidge's personal secretary, C. Bascom Slemp, defended the president. "Morning, noon, and night he keeps thinking, thinking," Slemp reported. "He indulges in no distracting pleasures."

Coolidge did find several ways to amuse himself, however. Every day Washington citizens could see the president strolling along with his bodyguard window-shopping, an activity he found relaxed his mind. For more physical exercise, he had a mechanical horse installed in the White House. While bouncing about on his electric steed, Coolidge sometimes even whooped like a cowboy. On Sundays the president regularly cruised on the Potomac River on the presidential yacht, *Mayflower*. During summer vacations in Wisconsin, Georgia, and South Dakota, Coolidge stood alongside lakes and streams with rod and reel and spent patient hours fishing.

Above: New York Yankee Babe Ruth at bat
Below: Explorer Richard Byrd with his Fokker plane

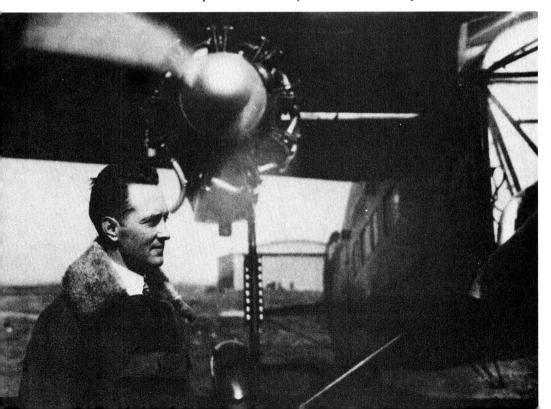

Above: Charles A. Lindbergh with the *Spirit of St. Louis*
Below: Coolidge fishing for trout in a Plymouth stream

Twice a week President Coolidge held press conferences. He understood the value of public relations and often allowed himself to be photographed. Coolidge loved animals, and newsmen snapped pictures of him with the pet dogs, cats, and even raccoon he kept at the White House. Visitors from all over the nation sometimes presented Coolidge with local costumes to wear. Friends objected that people were laughing at a picture of him dressed in a cowboy outfit, but Coolidge only responded, "Well, it's good for people to laugh." Once a silent newsreel cameraman hoped to get the president in action. "Look pleasant," he directed Coolidge, "and for Heaven's sake, say something—anything; good morning or howdy do!" In answer Coolidge dryly cracked, "That man gets more conversation out of me than all Congress."

As First Lady, Grace Coolidge easily displayed a natural gaiety and gracefulness that her husband lacked. One visiting society woman afterwards remembered Mrs. Coolidge's "genuine interest . . . which shone out through her warm, dark eyes, and her kindness [which] seemed to cast a sort of glow around her wherever she went." At official White House dinners, the First Lady always kept the conversation flowing smoothly while her husband generally sat in silence.

Even though he seemed to do little, President Coolidge remained very much in charge. "If you see ten troubles coming down the road," he once stated, "you can be sure that nine will run into a ditch before they reach you and you will have to do battle with only one of them." His cautious philosophy made him a popular president.

Above: Coolidge with the Sioux Indians in Deadwood, South Dakota
Below: Calvin, Grace, and their pets relax at The Beeches in Northampton.

By keeping well organized, Coolidge found it unnecessary to work long hours. "In the discharge of the duties of the office," he remarked, "there is one rule of action more important than all others. It consists in never doing anything that some one else can do for you." One day Secretary of Labor James J. Davis sent some documents to the president in order to get advice. "I am not going to read them," Coolidge curtly told the messenger. "You tell ol' man Davis I hired him as Secretary of Labor and if he can't do the job I'll get a new Secretary of Labor."

Certain matters, however, required Coolidge's thorough personal attention, and he did make a number of important decisions while president. Twice he vetoed Congress's McNary-Haugen Farm Bill, a bill designed to prop up agricultural prices at government expense. "Government price fixing," commented Coolidge, "once started, has alike no justice and no end. It is an economic folly from which this country has every right to be spared."

To combat interstate crime, Coolidge endorsed the reorganization of the Federal Bureau of Investigation. As its energetic new director, J. Edgar Hoover ordered government agents, soon called "G Men," to chase down federal criminals.

Coolidge boosted the American economy by cutting taxes and reducing the national debt. As a result, confident investors sank more and more borrowed money into Wall Street and watched the stock market zoom to dizzying heights. Some economists worried that this was an irresponsible and dangerous practice. Coolidge's advisers, however, believed that continued investment only aided

FBI director J. Edgar Hoover demonstrates the use of a machine gun.

the economy. The president, therefore, issued a number of public statements to encourage stock market advances.

In foreign affairs Coolidge left his mark also. South of the Rio Grande, Mexicans were ending many years of civil war. To establish good relations with Mexico, Coolidge sent Dwight Morrow to serve as U.S. ambassador. An Amherst classmate of Coolidge and a wealthy banker, Morrow successfully befriended the Mexican people by showing them he cared for their welfare.

To stabilize the shaky governments of the Central American nations of Honduras and Panama, Coolidge ordered U.S. Marines to those countries in 1924 and 1925. In 1926 U.S. Marines also landed in Nicaragua when a violent revolution erupted there. Coolidge summed up the situation by saying: "Whenever a condition of that kind exists in Central American countries, it means trouble for our citizens that are there and it is almost always necessary for this country to take action for their protection." The United States settled the Nicaraguan revolution through diplomatic channels, and peacekeeping American troops remained in that country until 1933.

In Europe, the horrible fighting of World War I had cost millions of lives. As Europeans cleaned up the rubble and tended the graves of loved ones, their governments prayed for a way to end all wars. Secretary of State Frank Kellogg suggested an international agreement as a means of settling future disputes. Together with French premier Aristide Briand, Kellogg organized a plan to outlaw war. On August 27, 1928, fifteen world nations signed the Kellogg-Briand Peace Pact in Paris, France. In support of the measure, President Coolidge announced, "It holds a greater hope for peaceful relations than was ever before given to the world."

Eventually forty-seven other countries also signed the peace accord. Unfortunately, in the years to come, dictators Adolf Hitler in Germany and Benito Mussolini in Italy showed no interest in obeying the pact. In 1939, World War II broke out as Europeans again took up arms against one another.

Above: The Coolidges in Havana, Cuba, with President Machado (right) and
Mrs. Machado (left).   Below: Coolidge signs the Kellogg-Briand Peace Pact.

Chapter 6

"I Do Not Choose to Run"

One day during a fresh-air walk with the president, Missouri senator Seldon Spencer gazed at the White House and teased, "I wonder who lives there?"

"Nobody," commented Coolidge, "they just come and go."

Long before the end of his term, Coolidge surprised the nation by announcing his own intention to go. On August 2, 1927, he stated with typical briefness, "I do not choose to run for President in 1928." But he refused to give his reasons for the decision. One persistent reporter asked, "Exactly why don't you want to be president again, Mr. Coolidge?" "Because," Coolidge sourly answered, brushing him aside, "there's no chance for advancement."

The president's Secret Service aide, Colonel Edmund Starling, believed he understood Coolidge's reasons. "The novelty of being President had worn off," Starling guessed, "the glory of it had gone with Calvin [Jr.'s] death; there was no great national crisis which demanded a continuation of his leadership. From now on the office was more of a burden than anything else. The steady grind of work was wearing him down. . . ."

Secretary of Commerce Herbert Hoover visiting President Coolidge

Many historians believe Coolidge also foresaw the dangers of too much reckless Wall Street investing. They think he simply did not wish to be in office when the stock market bubble burst. Grace Coolidge even revealed one day, "Poppa says there's a depression coming."

Whatever his motives, Coolidge took no part in the 1928 national election process. In June, Secretary of Commerce Herbert Hoover won the Republican presidential nomination. After a successful campaign against the Democratic nominee, New York governor Al Smith, Hoover was elected president on November 6, 1928.

As the end of his term neared, Coolidge organized the packing of his personal possessions. Assistants filled more than 150 boxes with the gifts Coolidge had received while

The Beeches, the Coolidges' estate in Northampton, Massachusetts

in office. "I am having rather more trouble in getting out of the White House," the president joked, "than I had getting in." On March 4, 1929, Coolidge attended the inauguration of Herbert Hoover, and that evening he boarded a northbound train and departed Washington.

The Coolidges retired to Northampton, Massachusetts, where they lived for a time in the same old rented two-family house on Massasoit Street. During the next months a constant stream of curious strangers drove past the simple house, and prying reporters often knocked at the door or gazed in through the windows. Finally, in the spring of 1930, Coolidge bought a handsome estate near Northampton called The Beeches. In this twelve-room house on nine secluded acres he enjoyed privacy and comfort.

Throngs of people outside the New York Stock Exchange on October 24, 1929

Coolidge maintained his law office in Northampton but did no law work. Instead, with free time on his hands, he penned his *Autobiography*. He served on the board of directors of the New York Life Insurance Company and sometimes wrote magazine articles on political subjects. For a time he also composed a newspaper column called "Thinking Things Over with Calvin Coolidge."

When the stock market suddenly crashed in October 1929, it plunged the United States into its deepest depression ever. Companies went bankrupt and factories laid off millions of laborers. Unemployed Americans walked the streets in a hopeless search for work. Some men sold pencils or apples on street corners to earn a few cents. Others tramped the countryside begging door-to-door. Women and children lined up at city soup kitchens to get a scrap to eat. Coolidge sadly observed the situation but could offer

Democratic presidential candidate Franklin D. Roosevelt

no real advice. The prosperity of his presidential years had disappeared. As the world swirled past him Coolidge told a friend, "I feel I no longer fit in with these times."

During the presidential campaign of 1932, Coolidge traveled to New York City to speak in support of Herbert Hoover's reelection. A large crowd at Madison Square Garden applauded Coolidge's words with enthusiasm. Later an excited woman approached the ex-president. "Oh, Mr. Coolidge," she exclaimed, "I enjoyed your speech so much that I stood up during the whole speech." With a straight face Coolidge responded, "So did I."

Coolidge's efforts in behalf of Herbert Hoover did little to help. American voters blamed Hoover for the Great Depression and desired immediate governmental change. In the November election they chose Democratic candidate Franklin D. Roosevelt.

After Hoover's defeat, sixty-year-old Coolidge returned to his quiet life-style in Northampton. "I feel I am more and more worn out," he soon wrote Colonel Starling. Often exhausted, on New Year's Day of 1933 he told a friend, "I am very comfortable because I am not doing anything of real account. But any effort to accomplish something goes hard with me. I am too old for my years. I suppose carrying responsibility takes its toll. I am afraid I am all burned out."

On the wintry morning of January 5, 1933, Coolidge rose early and ate breakfast. At nine o'clock he traveled downtown to examine his mail at his office, but he left early because he did not feel well. In the library at The Beeches he amused himself for a while by working on a jigsaw puzzle of George Washington. Later he went down into the cellar to watch the handyman stoke the furnace with coal.

At noon Coolidge remembered he had not shaved yet. He climbed upstairs and entered his bedroom and prepared his soap and razor. About an hour later Grace Coolidge went to fetch her husband for lunch. She discovered his lifeless body sprawled across the bathroom floor. He had died quietly and alone of a sudden heart attack.

Thousands of people gathered in Northampton on the cold, rainy day of Coolidge's memorial service. Many mourners followed the funeral procession that carried his body to its final resting place in the Coolidge family plot in Plymouth Notch. In one memorial speech Al Smith exclaimed that Coolidge left the nation "a shining public

Calvin Coolidge's casket in the Edwards Congregational Church, Northampton

example of the simple and homely virtues which came down to him from his New England ancestors." President Hoover stated, "Any summation of Mr. Coolidge's service to the country must conclude that America is a better place for his having lived in it."

Across the United States, people fondly remembered Silent Cal's dry wit, his curious habits, and his sense of dignity. As Americans toughened themselves for the difficult days that faced them, they missed Calvin Coolidge and the carefree times he represented.

**Above: Coolidge's grave in the Coolidge family lot in Plymouth, Vermont
Opposite page: Coolidge working in the hay fields on the family farm**

Chronology of American History

(Shaded area covers events in Calvin Coolidge's lifetime.)

About A.D. 982 — Eric the Red, born in Norway, reaches Greenland in one of the first European voyages to North America.

About 1000 — Leif Ericson (Eric the Red's son) leads what is thought to be the first European expedition to mainland North America; Leif probably lands in Canada.

1492 — Christopher Columbus, seeking a sea route from Spain to the Far East, discovers the New World.

1497 — John Cabot reaches Canada in the first English voyage to North America.

1513 — Ponce de Léon explores Florida in search of the fabled Fountain of Youth.

1519-1521 — Hernando Cortés of Spain conquers Mexico.

1534 — French explorers led by Jacques Cartier enter the Gulf of St. Lawrence in Canada.

1540 — Spanish explorer Francisco Coronado begins exploring the American Southwest, seeking the riches of the mythical Seven Cities of Cibola.

1565 — St. Augustine, Florida, the first permanent European town in what is now the United States, is founded by the Spanish.

1607 — Jamestown, Virginia, is founded, the first permanent English town in the present-day U.S.

1608 — Frenchman Samuel de Champlain founds the village of Quebec, Canada.

1609 — Henry Hudson explores the eastern coast of present-day U.S. for the Netherlands; the Dutch then claim parts of New York, New Jersey, Delaware, and Connecticut and name the area New Netherland.

1619 — The English colonies' first shipment of black slaves arrives in Jamestown.

1620 — English Pilgrims found Massachusetts' first permanent town at Plymouth.

1621 — Massachusetts Pilgrims and Indians hold the famous first Thanksgiving feast in colonial America.

1623 — Colonization of New Hampshire is begun by the English.

1624 — Colonization of present-day New York State is begun by the Dutch at Fort Orange (Albany).

1625 — The Dutch start building New Amsterdam (now New York City).

1630 — The town of Boston, Massachusetts, is founded by the English Puritans.

1633 — Colonization of Connecticut is begun by the English.

1634 — Colonization of Maryland is begun by the English.

1636 — Harvard, the colonies' first college, is founded in Massachusetts. Rhode Island colonization begins when Englishman Roger Williams founds Providence.

1638 — Delaware colonization begins as Swedes build Fort Christina at present-day Wilmington.

1640 — Stephen Daye of Cambridge, Massachusetts prints *The Bay Psalm Book*, the first English-language book published in what is now the U.S.

1643 — Swedish settlers begin colonizing Pennsylvania.

About 1650 — North Carolina is colonized by Virginia settlers.

1660 — New Jersey colonization is begun by the Dutch at present-day Jersey City.

1670 — South Carolina colonization is begun by the English near Charleston.

1673 — Jacques Marquette and Louis Jolliet explore the upper Mississippi River for France.

1682—Philadelphia, Pennsylvania, is settled. La Salle explores Mississippi River all the way to its mouth in Louisiana and claims the whole Mississippi Valley for France.

1693—College of William and Mary is founded in Williamsburg, Virginia.

1700—Colonial population is about 250,000.

1703—Benjamin Franklin is born in Boston.

1732—George Washington, first president of the U.S., is born in Westmoreland County, Virginia.

1733—James Oglethorpe founds Savannah, Georgia; Georgia is established as the thirteenth colony.

1735—John Adams, second president of the U.S., is born in Braintree, Massachusetts.

1737—William Byrd founds Richmond, Virginia.

1738—British troops are sent to Georgia over border dispute with Spain.

1739—Black insurrection takes place in South Carolina.

1740—English Parliament passes act allowing naturalization of immigrants to American colonies after seven-year residence.

1743—Thomas Jefferson is born in Albemarle County, Virginia. Benjamin Franklin retires at age thirty-seven to devote himself to scientific inquiries and public service.

1744—King George's War begins; France joins war effort against England.

1745—During King George's War, France raids settlements in Maine and New York.

1747—Classes begin at Princeton College in New Jersey.

1748—The Treaty of Aix-la-Chapelle concludes King George's War.

1749—Parliament legally recognizes slavery in colonies and the inauguration of the plantation system in the South. George Washington becomes the surveyor for Culpepper County in Virginia.

1750—Thomas Walker passes through and names Cumberland Gap on his way toward Kentucky region. Colonial population is about 1,200,000.

1751—James Madison, fourth president of the U.S., is born in Port Conway, Virginia. English Parliament passes Currency Act, banning New England colonies from issuing paper money. George Washington travels to Barbados.

1752—Pennsylvania Hospital, the first general hospital in the colonies, is founded in Philadelphia. Benjamin Franklin uses a kite in a thunderstorm to demonstrate that lightning is a form of electricity.

1753—George Washington delivers command that the French withdraw from the Ohio River Valley; French disregard the demand. Colonial population is about 1,328,000.

1754—French and Indian War begins (extends to Europe as the Seven Years' War). Washington surrenders at Fort Necessity.

1755—French and Indians ambush Braddock. Washington becomes commander of Virginia troops.

1756—England declares war on France.

1758—James Monroe, fifth president of the U.S., is born in Westmoreland County, Virginia.

1759—Cherokee Indian war begins in southern colonies; hostilities extend to 1761. George Washington marries Martha Dandridge Custis.

1760—George III becomes king of England. Colonial population is about 1,600,000.

1762—England declares war on Spain.

1763—Treaty of Paris concludes the French and Indian War and the Seven Years' War. England gains Canada and most other French lands east of the Mississippi River.

1764—British pass the Sugar Act to gain tax money from the colonists. The issue of taxation without representation is first introduced in Boston. John Adams marries Abigail Smith.

1765—Stamp Act goes into effect in the colonies. Business virtually stops as almost all colonists refuse to use the stamps.

1766—British repeal the Stamp Act.

1767—John Quincy Adams, sixth president of the U.S. and son of second president John Adams, is born in Braintree, Massachusetts. Andrew Jackson, seventh president of the U.S., is born in Waxhaw settlement, South Carolina.

1769—Daniel Boone sights the Kentucky Territory.

1770—In the Boston Massacre, British soldiers kill five colonists and injure six. Townshend Acts are repealed, thus eliminating all duties on imports to the colonies except tea.

1771—Benjamin Franklin begins his autobiography, a work that he will never complete. The North Carolina assembly passes the "Bloody Act," which makes rioters guilty of treason.

1772—Samuel Adams rouses colonists to consider British threats to self-government.

1773—English Parliament passes the Tea Act. Colonists dressed as Mohawk Indians board British tea ships and toss 342 casks of tea into the water in what becomes known as the Boston Tea Party. William Henry Harrison is born in Charles City County, Virginia.

1774—British close the port of Boston to punish the city for the Boston Tea Party. First Continental Congress convenes in Philadelphia.

1775—American Revolution begins with battles of Lexington and Concord, Massachusetts. Second Continental Congress opens in Philadelphia. George Washington becomes commander-in-chief of the Continental army.

1776—Declaration of Independence is adopted on July 4.

1777—Congress adopts the American flag with thirteen stars and thirteen stripes. John Adams is sent to France to negotiate peace treaty.

1778—France declares war against Great Britain and becomes U.S. ally.

1779—British surrender to Americans at Vincennes. Thomas Jefferson is elected governor of Virginia. James Madison is elected to the Continental Congress.

1780—Benedict Arnold, first American traitor, defects to the British.

1781—Articles of Confederation go into effect. Cornwallis surrenders to George Washington at Yorktown, ending the American Revolution.

1782—American commissioners, including John Adams, sign peace treaty with British in Paris. Thomas Jefferson's wife, Martha, dies. Martin Van Buren is born in Kinderhook, New York.

1784—Zachary Taylor is born near Barboursville, Virginia.

1785—Congress adopts the dollar as the unit of currency. John Adams is made minister to Great Britain. Thomas Jefferson is appointed minister to France.

1786—Shays's Rebellion begins in Massachusetts.

1787—Constitutional Convention assembles in Philadelphia, with George Washington presiding; U.S. Constitution is adopted. Delaware, New Jersey, and Pennsylvania become states.

1788—Virginia, South Carolina, New York, Connecticut, New Hampshire, Maryland, and Massachusetts become states. U.S. Constitution is ratified. New York City is declared U.S. capital.

1789—Presidential electors elect George Washington and John Adams as first president and vice-president. Thomas Jefferson is appointed secretary of state. North Carolina becomes a state. French Revolution begins.

1790—Supreme Court meets for the first time. Rhode Island becomes a state. First national census in the U.S. counts 3,929,214 persons. John Tyler is born in Charles City County, Virginia.

1791—Vermont enters the Union. U.S. Bill of Rights, the first ten amendments to the Constitution, goes into effect. District of Columbia is established. James Buchanan is born in Stony Batter, Pennsylvania.

1792—Thomas Paine publishes *The Rights of Man*. Kentucky becomes a state. Two political parties are formed in the U.S., Federalist and Republican. Washington is elected to a second term, with Adams as vice-president.

1793—War between France and Britain begins; U.S. declares neutrality. Eli Whitney invents the cotton gin; cotton production and slave labor increase in the South.

92

1794—Eleventh Amendment to the Constitution is passed, limiting federal courts' power. "Whiskey Rebellion" in Pennsylvania protests federal whiskey tax. James Madison marries Dolley Payne Todd.

1795—George Washington signs the Jay Treaty with Great Britain. Treaty of San Lorenzo, between U.S. and Spain, settles Florida boundary and gives U.S. right to navigate the Mississippi. James Polk is born near Pineville, North Carolina.

1796—Tennessee enters the Union. Washington gives his Farewell Address, refusing a third presidential term. John Adams is elected president and Thomas Jefferson vice-president.

1797—Adams recommends defense measures against possible war with France. Napoleon Bonaparte and his army march against Austrians in Italy. U.S. population is about 4,900,000.

1798—Washington is named commander-in-chief of the U.S. Army. Department of the Navy is created. Alien and Sedition Acts are passed. Napoleon's troops invade Egypt and Switzerland.

1799—George Washington dies at Mount Vernon, New York. James Monroe is elected governor of Virginia. French Revolution ends. Napoleon becomes ruler of France.

1800—Thomas Jefferson and Aaron Burr tie for president. U.S. capital is moved from Philadelphia to Washington, D.C. The White House is built as presidents' home. Spain returns Louisiana to France. Millard Fillmore is born in Locke, New York.

1801—After thirty-six ballots, House of Representatives elects Thomas Jefferson president, making Burr vice-president. James Madison is named secretary of state.

1802—Congress abolishes excise taxes. U.S. Military Academy is founded at West Point, New York.

1803—Ohio enters the Union. Louisiana Purchase treaty is signed with France, greatly expanding U.S. territory.

1804—Twelfth Amendment to the Constitution rules that president and vice-president be elected separately. Alexander Hamilton is killed by Vice-President Aaron Burr in a duel. Orleans Territory is established. Napoleon crowns himself emperor of France. Franklin Pierce is born in Hillsborough Lower Village, New Hampshire.

1805—Thomas Jefferson begins his second term as president. Lewis and Clark expedition reaches the Pacific Ocean.

1806—Coinage of silver dollars is stopped; resumes in 1836.

1807—Aaron Burr is acquitted in treason trial. Embargo Act closes U.S. ports to trade.

1808—James Madison is elected president. Congress outlaws importing slaves from Africa. Andrew Johnson is born in Raleigh, North Carolina.

1809—Abraham Lincoln is born near Hodgenville, Kentucky.

1810—U.S. population is 7,240,000.

1811—William Henry Harrison defeats Indians at Tippecanoe. Monroe is named secretary of state.

1812—Louisiana becomes a state. U.S. declares war on Britain (War of 1812). James Madison is reelected president. Napoleon invades Russia.

1813—British forces take Fort Niagara and Buffalo, New York.

1814—Francis Scott Key writes "The Star-Spangled Banner." British troops burn much of Washington, D.C., including the White House. Treaty of Ghent ends War of 1812. James Monroe becomes secretary of war.

1815—Napoleon meets his final defeat at Battle of Waterloo.

1816—James Monroe is elected president. Indiana becomes a state.

1817—Mississippi becomes a state. Construction on Erie Canal begins.

1818—Illinois enters the Union. The present thirteen-stripe flag is adopted. Border between U.S. and Canada is agreed upon.

1819—Alabama becomes a state. U.S. purchases Florida from Spain. Thomas Jefferson establishes the University of Virginia.

1820—James Monroe is reelected. In the Missouri Compromise, Maine enters the Union as a free (non-slave) state.

1821—Missouri enters the Union as a slave state. Santa Fe Trail opens the American Southwest. Mexico declares independence from Spain. Napoleon Bonaparte dies.

1822—U.S. recognizes Mexico and Colombia. Liberia in Africa is founded as a home for freed slaves. Ulysses S. Grant is born in Point Pleasant, Ohio. Rutherford B. Hayes is born in Delaware, Ohio.

1823—Monroe Doctrine closes North and South America to European colonizing or invasion.

1824—House of Representatives elects John Quincy Adams president when none of the four candidates wins a majority in national election. Mexico becomes a republic.

1825—Erie Canal is opened. U.S. population is 11,300,000.

1826—Thomas Jefferson and John Adams both die on July 4, the fiftieth anniversary of the Declaration of Independence.

1828—Andrew Jackson is elected president. Tariff of Abominations is passed, cutting imports.

1829—James Madison attends Virginia's constitutional convention. Slavery is abolished in Mexico. Chester A. Arthur is born in Fairfield, Vermont.

1830—Indian Removal Act to resettle Indians west of the Mississippi is approved.

1831—James Monroe dies in New York City. James A. Garfield is born in Orange, Ohio. Cyrus McCormick develops his reaper.

1832—Andrew Jackson, nominated by the new Democratic Party, is reelected president.

1833—Britain abolishes slavery in its colonies. Benjamin Harrison is born in North Bend, Ohio.

1835—Federal government becomes debt-free for the first time.

1836—Martin Van Buren becomes president. Texas wins independence from Mexico. Arkansas joins the Union. James Madison dies at Montpelier, Virginia.

1837—Michigan enters the Union. U.S. population is 15,900,000. Grover Cleveland is born in Caldwell, New Jersey.

1840—William Henry Harrison is elected president.

1841—President Harrison dies in Washington, D.C., one month after inauguration. Vice-President John Tyler succeeds him.

1843—William McKinley is born in Niles, Ohio.

1844—James Knox Polk is elected president. Samuel Morse sends first telegraphic message.

1845—Texas and Florida become states. Potato famine in Ireland causes massive emigration from Ireland to U.S. Andrew Jackson dies near Nashville, Tennessee.

1846—Iowa enters the Union. War with Mexico begins.

1847—U.S. captures Mexico City.

1848—Zachary Taylor becomes president. Treaty of Guadalupe Hidalgo ends Mexico-U.S. war. Wisconsin becomes a state.

1849—James Polk dies in Nashville, Tennessee.

1850—President Taylor dies in Washington, D.C.; Vice-President Millard Fillmore succeeds him. California enters the Union, breaking tie between slave and free states.

1852—Franklin Pierce is elected president.

1853—Gadsden Purchase transfers Mexican territory to U.S.

1854—"War for Bleeding Kansas" is fought between slave and free states.

1855—Czar Nicholas I of Russia dies, succeeded by Alexander II.

1856—James Buchanan is elected president. In Massacre of Potawatomi Creek, Kansas-slavers are murdered by free-staters. Woodrow Wilson is born in Staunton, Virginia.

1857—William Howard Taft is born in Cincinnati, Ohio.

1858—Minnesota enters the Union. Theodore Roosevelt is born in New York City.

1859—Oregon becomes a state.

1860—Abraham Lincoln is elected president; South Carolina secedes from the Union in protest.

1861—Arkansas, Tennessee, North Carolina, and Virginia secede. Kansas enters the Union as a free state. Civil War begins.

1862—Union forces capture Fort Henry, Roanoke Island, Fort Donelson, Jacksonville, and New Orleans; Union armies are defeated at the battles of Bull Run and Fredericksburg. Martin Van Buren dies in Kinderhook, New York. John Tyler dies near Charles City, Virginia.

1863—Lincoln issues Emancipation Proclamation: all slaves held in rebelling territories are declared free. West Virginia becomes a state.

1864—Abraham Lincoln is reelected. Nevada becomes a state.

1865—Lincoln is assassinated in Washington, D.C., and succeeded by Andrew Johnson. U.S. Civil War ends on May 26. Thirteenth Amendment abolishes slavery. Warren G. Harding is born in Blooming Grove, Ohio.

1867—Nebraska becomes a state. U.S. buys Alaska from Russia for $7,200,000. Reconstruction Acts are passed.

1868—President Johnson is impeached for violating Tenure of Office Act, but is acquitted by Senate. Ulysses S. Grant is elected president. Fourteenth Amendment prohibits voting discrimination. James Buchanan dies in Lancaster, Pennsylvania.

1869—Franklin Pierce dies in Concord, New Hampshire.

1870—Fifteenth Amendment gives blacks the right to vote.

1872—Grant is reelected over Horace Greeley. General Amnesty Act pardons ex-Confederates. Calvin Coolidge is born in Plymouth Notch, Vermont.

1874—Millard Fillmore dies in Buffalo, New York. Herbert Hoover is born in West Branch, Iowa.

1875—Andrew Johnson dies in Carter's Station, Tennessee.

1876—Colorado enters the Union. "Custer's last stand": he and his men are massacred by Sioux Indians at Little Big Horn, Montana.

1877—Rutherford B. Hayes is elected president as all disputed votes are awarded to him.

1880—James A. Garfield is elected president.

1881—President Garfield is assassinated and dies in Elberon, New Jersey. Vice-President Chester A. Arthur succeeds him.

1882—U.S. bans Chinese immigration. Franklin D. Roosevelt is born in Hyde Park, New York.

1884—Grover Cleveland is elected president. Harry S. Truman is born in Lamar, Missouri.

1885—Ulysses S. Grant dies in Mount McGregor, New York.

1886—Statue of Liberty is dedicated. Chester A. Arthur dies in New York City.

1888—Benjamin Harrison is elected president.

1889—North Dakota, South Dakota, Washington, and Montana become states.

1890—Dwight D. Eisenhower is born in Denison, Texas. Idaho and Wyoming become states.

1892—Grover Cleveland is elected president.

1893—Rutherford B. Hayes dies in Fremont, Ohio.

1896—William McKinley is elected president. Utah becomes a state.

1898—U.S. declares war on Spain over Cuba.

1900—McKinley is reelected. Boxer Rebellion against foreigners in China begins.

1901—McKinley is assassinated by anarchist Leon Czolgosz in Buffalo, New York; Theodore Roosevelt becomes president. Benjamin Harrison dies in Indianapolis, Indiana.

1902—U.S. acquires perpetual control over Panama Canal.

1903—Alaskan frontier is settled.

1904—Russian-Japanese War breaks out. Theodore Roosevelt wins presidential election.

1905—Treaty of Portsmouth signed, ending Russian-Japanese War.

1906—U.S. troops occupy Cuba.

1907—President Roosevelt bars all Japanese immigration. Oklahoma enters the Union.

1908—William Howard Taft becomes president. Grover Cleveland dies in Princeton, New Jersey. Lyndon B. Johnson is born near Stonewall, Texas.

1909—NAACP is founded under W.E.B. DuBois

1910—China abolishes slavery.

1911—Chinese Revolution begins. Ronald Reagan is born in Tampico, Illinois.

1912—Woodrow Wilson is elected president. Arizona and New Mexico become states.

1913—Federal income tax is introduced in U.S. through the Sixteenth Amendment. Richard Nixon is born in Yorba Linda, California. Gerald Ford is born in Omaha, Nebraska.

1914—World War I begins.

1915—British liner *Lusitania* is sunk by German submarine.

1916—Wilson is reelected president.

1917—U.S. breaks diplomatic relations with Germany. Czar Nicholas of Russia abdicates as revolution begins. U.S. declares war on Austria-Hungary. John F. Kennedy is born in Brookline, Massachusetts.

1918—Wilson proclaims "Fourteen Points" as war aims. On November 11, armistice is signed between Allies and Germany.

1919—Eighteenth Amendment prohibits sale and manufacture of intoxicating liquors. Wilson presides over first League of Nations; wins Nobel Peace Prize. Theodore Roosevelt dies in Oyster Bay, New York.

1920—Nineteenth Amendment (women's suffrage) is passed. Warren Harding is elected president.

1921—Adolf Hitler's stormtroopers begin to terrorize political opponents.

1922—Irish Free State is established. Soviet states form USSR. Benito Mussolini forms Fascist government in Italy.

1923—President Harding dies in San Francisco, California; he is succeeded by Vice-President Calvin Coolidge.

1924—Coolidge is elected president. Woodrow Wilson dies in Washington, D.C. James Carter is born in Plains, Georgia. George Bush is born in Milton, Massachusetts.

1925—Hitler reorganizes Nazi Party and publishes first volume of *Mein Kampf.*

1926—Fascist youth organizations founded in Germany and Italy. Republic of Lebanon proclaimed.

1927—Stalin becomes Soviet dictator. Economic conference in Geneva attended by fifty-two nations.

1928—Herbert Hoover is elected president. U.S. and many other nations sign Kellogg-Briand pacts to outlaw war.

1929—Stock prices in New York crash on "Black Thursday"; the Great Depression begins.

1930—Bank of U.S. and its many branches close (most significant bank failure of the year). William Howard Taft dies in Washington, D.C.

1931—Emigration from U.S. exceeds immigration for first time as Depression deepens.

1932—Franklin D. Roosevelt wins presidential election in a Democratic landslide.

1933—First concentration camps are erected in Germany. U.S. recognizes USSR and resumes trade. Twenty-First Amendment repeals prohibition. Calvin Coolidge dies in Northampton, Massachusetts.

1934—Severe dust storms hit Plains states. President Roosevelt passes U.S. Social Security Act.

1936—Roosevelt is reelected. Spanish Civil War begins. Hitler and Mussolini form Rome-Berlin Axis.

1937—Roosevelt signs Neutrality Act.

1938—Roosevelt sends appeal to Hitler and Mussolini to settle European problems amicably.

1939—Germany takes over Czechoslovakia and invades Poland, starting World War II.

1940—Roosevelt is reelected for a third term.

1941—Japan bombs Pearl Harbor, U.S. declares war on Japan. Germany and Italy declare war on U.S.; U.S. then declares war on them.

1942—Allies agree not to make separate peace treaties with the enemies. U.S. government transfers more than 100,000 Nisei (Japanese-Americans) from west coast to inland concentration camps.

1943—Allied bombings of Germany begin.

1944—Roosevelt is reelected for a fourth term. Allied forces invade Normandy on D-Day.

1945—President Franklin D. Roosevelt dies in Warm Springs, Georgia; Vice-President Harry S. Truman succeeds him. Mussolini is killed; Hitler commits suicide. Germany surrenders. U.S. drops atomic bomb on Hiroshima; Japan surrenders: end of World War II.

1946—U.N. General Assembly holds its first session in London. Peace conference of twenty-one nations is held in Paris.

1947—Peace treaties are signed in Paris. "Cold War" is in full swing.

1948—U.S. passes Marshall Plan Act, providing $17 billion in aid for Europe. U.S. recognizes new nation of Israel. India and Pakistan become free of British rule. Truman is elected president.

1949—Republic of Eire is proclaimed in Dublin. Russia blocks land route access from Western Germany to Berlin; airlift begins. U.S., France, and Britain agree to merge their zones of occupation in West Germany. Apartheid program begins in South Africa.

1950—Riots in Johannesburg, South Africa, against apartheid. North Korea invades South Korea. U.N. forces land in South Korea and recapture Seoul.

1951—Twenty-Second Amendment limits president to two terms.

1952—Dwight D. Eisenhower resigns as supreme commander in Europe and is elected president.

1953—Stalin dies; struggle for power in Russia follows. Rosenbergs are executed for espionage.

1954—U.S. and Japan sign mutual defense agreement.

1955—Blacks in Montgomery, Alabama, boycott segregated bus lines.

1956—Eisenhower is reelected president. Soviet troops march into Hungary.

1957—U.S. agrees to withdraw ground forces from Japan. Russia launches first satellite, *Sputnik.*

1958—European Common Market comes into being. Fidel Castro begins war against Batista government in Cuba.

1959—Alaska becomes the forty-ninth state. Hawaii becomes fiftieth state. Castro becomes premier of Cuba. De Gaulle is proclaimed president of the Fifth Republic of France.

1960—Historic debates between Senator John F. Kennedy and Vice-President Richard Nixon are televised. Kennedy is elected president. Brezhnev becomes president of USSR.

1961—Berlin Wall is constructed. Kennedy and Khrushchev confer in Vienna. In Bay of Pigs incident, Cubans trained by CIA attempt to overthrow Castro.

1962—U.S. military council is established in South Vietnam.

1963—Riots and beatings by police and whites mark civil rights demonstrations in Birmingham, Alabama; 30,000 troops are called out, Martin Luther King, Jr., is arrested. Freedom marchers descend on Washington, D.C., to demonstrate. President Kennedy is assassinated in Dallas, Texas; Vice-President Lyndon B. Johnson is sworn in as president.

1964—U.S. aircraft bomb North Vietnam. Johnson is elected president. Herbert Hoover dies in New York City.

1965—U.S. combat troops arrive in South Vietnam.

1966—Thousands protest U.S. policy in Vietnam. National Guard quells race riots in Chicago.

1967—Six-Day War between Israel and Arab nations.

1968—Martin Luther King, Jr., is assassinated in Memphis, Tennessee. Senator Robert Kennedy is assassinated in Los Angeles. Riots and police brutality take place at Democratic National Convention in Chicago. Richard Nixon is elected president. Czechoslovakia is invaded by Soviet troops.

1969—Dwight D. Eisenhower dies in Washington, D.C. Hundreds of thousands of people in several U.S. cities demonstrate against Vietnam War.

1970—Four Vietnam War protesters are killed by National Guardsmen at Kent State University in Ohio.

1971—Twenty-Sixth Amendment allows eighteen-year-olds to vote.

1972—Nixon visits Communist China; is reelected president in near-record landslide. Watergate affair begins when five men are arrested in the Watergate hotel complex in Washington, D.C. Nixon announces resignations of aides Haldeman, Ehrlichman, and Dean and Attorney General Kleindienst as a result of Watergate-related charges. Harry S. Truman dies in Kansas City, Missouri.

1973—Vice-President Spiro Agnew resigns; Gerald Ford is named vice-president. Vietnam peace treaty is formally approved after nineteen months of negotiations. Lyndon B. Johnson dies in San Antonio, Texas.

1974—As a result of Watergate cover-up, impeachment is considered; Nixon resigns and Ford becomes president. Ford pardons Nixon and grants limited amnesty to Vietnam War draft evaders and military deserters.

1975—U.S. civilians are evacuated from Saigon, South Vietnam, as Communist forces complete takeover of South Vietnam.

1976—U.S. celebrates its Bicentennial. James Earl Carter becomes president.

1977—Carter pardons most Vietnam draft evaders, numbering some 10,000.

1980—Ronald Reagan is elected president.

1981—President Reagan is shot in the chest in assassination attempt. Sandra Day O'Connor is appointed first woman justice of the Supreme Court.

1983—U.S. troops invade island of Grenada.

1984—Reagan is reelected president. Democratic candidate Walter Mondale's running mate, Geraldine Ferraro, is the first woman selected for vice-president by a major U.S. political party.

1985—Soviet Communist Party secretary Konstantin Chernenko dies; Mikhail Gorbachev succeeds him. U.S. and Soviet officials discuss arms control in Geneva. Reagan and Gorbachev hold summit conference in Geneva. Racial tensions accelerate in South Africa.

1986—Space shuttle *Challenger* explodes shortly after takeoff; crew of seven dies. U.S. bombs bases in Libya. Corazon Aquino defeats Ferdinand Marcos in Philippine presidential election.

1987—Iraqi missile rips the U.S. frigate *Stark* in the Persian Gulf, killing thirty-seven American sailors. Congress holds hearings to investigate sale of U.S. arms to Iran to finance Nicaraguan *contra* movement.

1988—President Reagan and Soviet leader Gorbachev sign INF treaty, eliminating intermediate nuclear forces. Severe drought sweeps the United States. George Bush is elected president.

1989—East Germany opens Berlin Wall, allowing citizens free exit. Communists lose control of governments in Poland, Romania, and Czechoslovakia. Chinese troops massacre over 1,000 pro-democracy student demonstrators in Beijing's Tiananmen Square.

1990—Iraq annexes Kuwait, provoking the threat of war. East and West Germany are reunited. The Cold War between the United States and the Soviet Union comes to a close. Several Soviet republics make moves toward independence.

1991—Backed by a coalition of members of the United Nations, U.S. troops drive Iraqis from Kuwait. Latvia, Lithuania, and Estonia withdraw from the USSR. The Soviet Union dissolves as its republics secede to form a Commonwealth of Independent States.

1992—U.N. forces fail to stop fighting in territories of former Yugoslavia. More than fifty people are killed and more than six hundred buildings burned in rioting in Los Angeles. U.S. unemployment reaches eight-year high. Hurricane Andrew devastates southern Florida and parts of Louisiana. International relief supplies and troops are sent to combat famine and violence in Somalia.

1993—U.S.-led forces use airplanes and missiles to attack military targets in Iraq. William Jefferson Clinton becomes the forty-second U.S. president.

1994—Richard M. Nixon dies in New York City.

Index

Page numbers in boldface type indicate illustrations.

Adams House (hotel), 28, 32, 37, 43, 45
agriculture, 76
Alaska, 50
alcohol, 68
Amherst College, 20-22, **22**, 77
Atlantic Ocean, 70
attorney general, U.S., 57
Austria-Hungary, 34
Autobiography (Coolidge's), 84
automobiles, 68
aviation, 70
baseball, 70, **72**
Beeches, The (home of Coolidge), 83, **83**
Bennett, Floyd, 70
Bennington, Vermont, 20
Bible, 67-68
birthplace, of Coolidge, **4**
Black River Academy, 18-20, **20**
Borah, William, 57
Boston, Massachusetts, 27-28, 35, 37, 39-43, 45, 50
Briand, Aristide, 78
Bridgewater, Vermont, 7
Brown, Carrie A., 21
Bryan, William Jennings, **69**
Byrd, Richard, 70, **72**
cabinet (presidential advisers), 48, 56, **56**
California, 42, 48
Capitol, U.S., 48, 67
Capone, Al, 68
cartoons, **58**
Central America, 78
characteristics, of Coolidge, 11, 15, 19, 21, 34-35, 47, 49, 62, 70, 87
Chicago, Illinois, 42, 44, 68
childhood, Coolidge's, 13-15, **15**, 16-17
Coolidge, Abigail (sister), 15, 19, **19**
Coolidge, Calvin, Jr. (son), 28, 37, 52, **53**, 55, 61, **62**, 64, 81
Coolidge, Calvin, photographs/pictures of, **2**, **6**, **9**, **10**, **11**, **12**, **15**, **17**, **20**, **22**, **24**, **29**, **30**, **34**, **36**, **40**, **45**, **46**, **54**, **55**, **56**, **60**, **62**, **63**, **64**, **66**, **73**, **75**, **79**, **80**, **82**, **88**
Coolidge, Calvin Galusha (grandfather), 17
Coolidge, Carrie Brown (stepmother), 21, **64**
Coolidge, Grace Goodhue (wife), 8, 10, 25-26, **27**, 37, 45, **54**, **62**, 64, **65**, **66**, 74, **75**, **79**, 82, 86
Coolidge, John (father), 7-9, **9**, 13-14, 16, 21-28, 51-53, **62**, **64**
Coolidge, John (son), 26, 37, **53**, 55, **62**, 64
Coolidge, Victoria Moor (mother), 13, **14**, 15, 18, 53

Congress, U.S., **48**, 76
Constitution, U.S., 9, 47, 67
Cox, Channing, 49
Cox, James, 47
Crane, Murray, 33
Curtis, Edward, 39, 41
Dale, Porter, 9
Darrown, Clarence, 68, **69**
Darwin, Charles, 68
Daugherty, Harry, 57, **58**
Davis, James, 76
Davis, John W., 60
Dawes, Charles, 59, **60**, **63**, **66**
death, of Coolidge, 86-87, **87**
demonstrations, **38**, 39, 40, **40**
Denby, Edwin, 57, **57**
economy, U.S., 76, 84-85
education, Coolidge's, 15, 18, 20-22
England, 34
Europe, 78
evolution, theory of, 68
Fall, Albert B., 56-57, **58**
Federal Bureau of Investigation, 76
Ford, Henry, 68
France, 34, 37, 78
Garman, Charles E., 21
Georgia, 71
Germany, 34, 78
"G Men," 76
Gillet, Frederick, 43
Gompers, Samuel, 41, **41**
governor, of Massachusetts, 35-42
Great Depression, 85
Hammond and Field (law firm), 23-24
Harding, Warren G., 7-8, 11, 43-44, 47-48, 50-52, 54, 56
Harrison, Benjamin, 20
Have Faith in Massachusetts (book), 42
Hitler, Adolph, 78
homes, of Coolidge, 7, 26, **51**, 83, **83**
Honduras, 78
Hoover, Herbert, 82, **82**, 83, 85-87
Hoover, J. Edgar, 76, **77**
housing shortages, 38
Hughes, Charles Evan, 8
Illinois, 42, 50, 59
inauguration, Coolidge's, **5**, **66**, 67
Indians, **75**
Irwin, Richard, 27
Italy, 34, 78
Jazz Singer, The (movie), 70
Jolson, Al, 70
Kellogg-Briand Peace Pact, 78
Kellogg, Frank, 78

La Follette, Robert, 60, **61**, 63
labor movement, 38-41
legal career, Coolidge's 23-26
legislature, Massachusetts, 28, 31-33
Lenroot, Irvine L., 44
lieutenant governor, of Massachusetts,
    33-35
Lindbergh, Charles, 70, **73**
Lodge, Henry Cabot, 51
Longworth, Alice Roosevelt, 55
Lowden, Frank, 42-43
Ludlow, 18, 19
Machado, President, of Cuba, **79**
Maine, 48
Marx, Groucho, 71
Massachusetts, 21, 23-25, 27-28, 31-45,
    50-51, 83, 84, 86
Mayflower (presidential yacht), 71
McCall, Samuel, 33-34, **34**
McNary-Haugen Farm Bill, 76
Mencken, H. L., 71
Mexico, 77
military, U.S., 37, **37**, 38-40, 78
Morrow, Dwight, 77
Mussolini, Benito, 78
newspapers, 8, **11**, 39-41, 63
New York, New York, 60, 70, 85
New York Stock Exchange, **84**
Nineteenth Amendment, 47
North Pole, 70
Northampton, Massachusetts, 23, 25,
    27-28, 31, 36-37, 83, **83**, 84, 86
Ohio, 43, 59
Oregon, 44
Peters, Andrew, 40
Plymouth Notch, Vermont, 7-8, 11, 13, 19,
    21, 51, **51**, 52, 86
police department, Boston, 39-40, **40**, 41-42
political conventions, 44, **44**, 60
political parties, 24-25, 27-28, 31, 33,
    35-36, 43, 45, 47, 59-62, 82, 85
Potomac River, 71
presidential elections, 47, 59-60, **60**, 61,
    62, 82
press conferences, 74
Prohibition, 62, 68
railroads, 32

Revolutionary War, American, 23
Rio Grande River, 77
"Roaring Twenties," 68
Roosevelt, Franklin Delano, 47, 85, **85**
Roosevelt, Theodore, 55
Ruth, Babe, 70, **72**
San Francisco, California, 51
schoolhouse, **16**
Seattle, Washington, 50
Secret Service, 81
Secretary: of Commerce, 82; of Labor, 76;
    of State, 8, 78; of the Interior, 56-57; of
    the Navy, 56-57
Senate, U.S., 45, 48, 50
"Silent Cal," 11, 49, 87
Slemp, C. Bascom, 71
Smith, Al, 82, 86
Smoot, Reed, 43
South Dakota, 71
South Pole, 70
Spencer, Seldon, 81
Spirit of St. Louis (airplane), 70
Stearns, Frank, 42
stock market, 76-77, 82, 84
Supreme Court, U.S., 56
Taft, Howard, 11, 56, 59, 67
taxes, 76
"Teapot Dome" scandal, 56-57, **58**, 59
Tennessee, 68
"Thinking Things Over with Calvin
    Coolidge" (newspaper column), 84
"Tin Lizzie," 68
tombstone, of Coolidge, **89**
Vermont, 7-8, 10-11, 13-14, 18-19, 21, 26,
    50-52, 86
vice-president, U.S., 43, 45, 50
Volstead Act, 54, 68
Wall Street, 76, 82
Washington, D.C., 48-50, 53, 67, 71
White House, 50, 54-55, 59, 61, 71, 81, 83
Wilson, Woodrow, 41
Wisconsin, 44, 60, 71
women's rights, 47
Wood, Leonard, 42-43
World War I, 34, 37, **37**, 68, 78
World War II, 78
Wyoming, 56

About the Author

Zachary Kent grew up in Little Falls, New Jersey, and received an English degree from St.
Lawrence University. Following college he worked at a New York City literary agency for two
years and then launched his writing career. To support himself while writing, he has worked
as a taxi driver, a shipping clerk, and a house painter. Mr. Kent has had a lifelong interest in
American history. Studying the U.S. presidents was his childhood hobby. His collection of
presidential items includes books, pictures, and games, as well as several autographed letters.